# MARTIN CLASSICAL LECTURES

*Martin Classical Lectures*

THESE LECTURES ARE DELIVERED ANNUALLY
AT OBERLIN COLLEGE
ON A FOUNDATION ESTABLISHED IN HONOR OF
CHARLES BEEBE MARTIN

# Society and Civilization in Greece and Rome

MARTIN CLASSICAL LECTURES
VOLUME XVIII

*by*

VICTOR EHRENBERG

-

PUBLISHED FOR OBERLIN COLLEGE
BY HARVARD UNIVERSITY PRESS
CAMBRIDGE, MASSACHUSETTS

1964

TO THE MEMORY OF

*Werner Jaeger*

Le secret d'être ennuyeux, c'est de tout dire

Voltaire

Einzig das Lied überm Land
heiligt und feiert

Rilke, *Sonette an Orpheus*

# *Preface*

When I was asked to deliver the Martin Lectures for 1962 at Oberlin College, it was suggested that at least in part I should talk on Rome. I felt I had to accept that condition, although I was a little uneasy about it. After all, my greater knowledge, as far as it goes, and my greater love, are clearly on the Greek side. Still, I did accept and have had to bear the consequences—along with my audience—and now with my readers.

I had planned, originally, to speak about "some aspects" of the interconnection between society and civilization. This would have been not a beautiful but a more modest and, therefore, more appropriate title. However, while working on my lectures, I was driven more and more toward an attempt at seeing the whole in the parts. This was a challenge which, as I myself knew best, could be met only insufficiently; but at my age the temptation to finish a small book rather than not to finish a large one was too great. Thus, I decided not to extend the scope of the book beyond that of my four lectures though the permission to do so was generously granted. Naturally, as I say in the first lecture, I have had to be very selective. I have excluded the Hellenistic and the Roman Imperial Ages largely because their universal civilizations were so very different from those of the city states. Moreover, not only am I too little of an expert on the Roman Empire, but there are the two great works by Michael Rostovtzeff with which only a giant could hope to compete. In general, I should like to ask my critics not to complain of what is absent or too briefly treated, but to criticize what is here, and to examine my claim of covering the essential aspects of my subject.

I dare hope that this may prove to be a book for both scholars and non-scholars, scholarly enough for the former and yet readable enough for the latter. Scholarship is not possible without analytical research, but imaginative synthesis is equally necessary. This must be the excuse, if excuse is needed, for the shape of this book. There is one other point. Lectures, in my view, should remain lectures even in print. This is one of the reasons why I have left my lectures practically unchanged, except for a number of small extensions either left out when I lectured, or added afterwards. For the same reason, there are no footnotes. They are a bookish matter, and not reconcilable with the spoken word. Scholars —and the present writer is no exception—are usually keen on seeing their own views quoted and discussed. That is only human, but we ought to learn that such procedure does not interest anybody outside the small body of "initiates." I hope my fellow scholars will be satisfied with the selected bibliography at the end of the book. Some source references are given in the text, others can be found easily in the books mentioned.

In dedicating this book to the memory of Werner Jaeger, I wish to acknowledge my debt to the author of *Paideia;* it will remain a great book, however strongly one may differ from some of its leading ideas or their application. At the same time, I wish to remember the hours my wife and I were allowed to spend with Jaeger and his wife when we were staying in Cambridge, Massachusetts, in 1958. We had been looking forward to seeing him again in 1962, and to experiencing once more his warm humanity and a friendship of which we were very proud. That was not to be.

I want to thank Oberlin College, and, in particular, Professor Charles T. Murphy, for giving me the opportunity of delivering these lectures and of spending ten delightful days at Oberlin. I wish also to thank the Institute for Advanced Study at Princeton for allowing me to spend a month there in order to put some final touches to my lectures and to enjoy the advantages both personal and scholarly of that unique research institute. A number of my friends have been very helpful in discussing various points with me; Professors J. Heurgon and O. Skutsch, in particular, saved me from some errors in Chapter IV. My sincere thanks are due to them as well as again to Professor Murphy, who kindly read my typescript, and to the anonymous scholar who read it for the publishers; both provided helpful suggestions and corrections. For their valuable help in my search for photographs, I want to thank Professors E. Kunze, F. Matz, Homer A. Thompson, T. B. L. Webster, and above all, P. E. Corbett. The staffs of various museums and institutes proved very helpful also. To members of the Harvard University Press I owe thanks for the great trouble they took over the editing and producing of this book.

V. E.

London, Summer 1963.

# Contents

## ILLUSTRATIONS

For permission to publish the illustrations, acknowledgments are due to the following: American School of Classical Studies, Athens; Deutsches archaeologisches Institut, Athens; Staatliche Museen, Berlin; The Trustees of the British Museum, London; Institute of Classical Studies, University of London; Archaeologisches Seminar, University of Marburg; Bildarchiv Foto, Marburg; Staatliche Antikensammlungen, Munich; Metropolitan Museum of Art, New York; Musée du Louvre, Paris; Cabinet des Médailles, Paris; Deutsches archaeologisches Institut, Rome; Fototeca di architettura e topografia dell'Italia antica, Rome.

FIGURE 1. Tiryns. Map of the upper citadel. Mostly late Helladic III (c. 1400–1200 B.C.). Shows the enormous strength of the fortifications and the two megara of the palace (M, O). Photo: Deutsches archaeologisches Institut, Athens.

FIGURE 2. Mycenae. Interior of beehive tomb ("Treasury of Atreus"). Late Helladic III. Photo: Bildarchiv Foto Marburg no. 134445.

FIGURE 3. Cnossus. Fresco: bull game with male and female athletes. Late Minoan I (c. 1550–1450 B.C.). Herakleion, Museum. Photo: Institute of Classical Studies, London.

FIGURE 4. Cnossus. Fresco: ladies as spectators. Late Minoan I. Herakleion, Museum. Photo: Institute of Classical Studies, London.

FIGURE 5. Hagia Triada. Sarcophagus. Procession with lyre-player. Late Minoan III (c. 1400 B.C.). Herakleion, Museum. Photo: Institute of Classical Studies, London.

FIGURE 6. Cnossus. Fayence. Minoan goddess (or priestess?) with snakes. Middle Minoan III (c. 1600 B.C.). Herakleion, Museum. Photo: Archaeologisches Seminar, University of Marburg.

FIGURE 7. Dipylon Oenochoe. Frieze with Aktorione-Moleone (*Il.* 11.709), fighting twins in one body. Second half of eighth century B.C. Photo: Agora Excavations, American School of Classical Studies, Athens.

FIGURE 8. Dipylon Krater. Funeral; chariots with warriors in procession. Second half of eighth century B.C. Metropolitan Museum of Art, New York, Rogers Fund 1914, no. 14.130.15. Photo: Museum.

FIGURE 9. Dipylon Krater. Funeral; fight over beached ship. Second half of eighth century B.C. Metropolitan Museum of Art, New York, Fletcher Fund 1934, no. 34.11.2. Photo: Museum.

FIGURE 10. Dipylon Oenochoe. Shipwreck (of Odysseus?). Second half of eighth century B.C. Munich no. 8696. Photo: Staatliche Antikensammlungen, Munich.

c. 490–480 B.C. Sparta, Museum. Photo: Deutsches archaeologisches Institut, Athens.

FIGURE 26. Attic tombstone. Thraseas and Euandria. Middle fourth century B.C. Berlin no. K 34. Photo: Staatliche Museen, Berlin.

FIGURE 27. Attic rf. Amphora. Comic chorus of knights. Middle sixth century B.C. Berlin no. F 1697. Photo: Staatliche Museen, Berlin.

FIGURE 28. Etruscan Bronze, fibula Praenestina. Second half of seventh century B.C. (CIL XIV 4123). Rome, Museo Preistorico. Photo: Gabinetto Fotografico Nazionale.

FIGURE 29. Etruscan Bronze. She-wolf, sixth/fifth century B.C. Rome, Museo dei Conservatori. Photo: Alinari no. 6042 C.

FIGURE 30. Etruscan Terracotta Sarcophagus. Married couple. Second half of sixth century B.C. Rome, Museo Villa Giulia. Photo: Alinari no. 53084.

FIGURE 31. Etruscan head, from sarcophagus. Third century B.C. Tarquinia, Museo Nazionale no. 9804. Photo: Deutsches archaeologisches Institut, Rome.

FIGURE 32. Roman portrait. Marble, first century B.C. Metropolitan Museum of Art, New York, Rogers Fund 1921, no. 21.88.11. Photo: Museum.

*The Martin Classical Lectures*

VOLUME XVIII

The Martin Foundation,
on which these lectures are delivered,
was established by his many friends in honor of
Charles Beebe Martin,
for forty-five years a teacher of classical literature
and classical art in Oberlin College.

## ABBREVIATIONS

Bruns   *Fontes Iuris Romani Antiqui,* ed. C. G. Bruns, 7 ed. edited by O. Gradenwitz (Tubingen: Mohr, 1909).

D   *Anthologia Lyrica Graeca,* ed. E. Diehl, 2 and 3 ed. (Leipzig: Teubner, 1942, 1954).

Dessau   *Inscriptiones Latinae Selectae,* ed. H. Dessau, vol. I (Berlin: Weidmann, 1892).

FGrH   *Die Fragmente der griechischen Historiker,* by F. Jacoby, part I, 2 ed. (Leiden: Brill, 1957); part II (Leiden: Brill, 1926).

K   *Comicorum Atticorum Fragmenta,* ed. Th. Kock, vol. I (Leipzig: Teubner, 1880).

L-P   *Poetarum Lesbiorum Fragmenta,* ed. E. Lobel and D. Page (Oxford: Clarendon Press, 1955).

P   *Poetae Melici Graeci,* ed. D. Page (Oxford: Clarendon Press, 1962).

Tod   *A Selection of Greek Historical Inscriptions,* ed. M. N. Tod, vol. I, 2 ed. (Oxford: Clarendon Press, 1946).

V   *Ennianae Poesis Reliquiae,* rec. J. Vahlen, 2 ed. (Leipzig: Teubner, 1928).

VS   *Die Fragmente der Vorsokratiker,* ed. H. Diels, 6 ed. edited by W. Kranz (Berlin: Weidmann, 1952).

# I. The Age of the Singers

It seems almost superfluous to say that my theme is far more comprehensive than anything I can deal with in a few lectures. If all writing of history must be selective, this is even more true of lecturing when one is bound to a time limit which must correspond to the limited capacity of an audience to listen. I shall have to be selective, not only within every period or society, but chiefly in the over-all picture. Every selection is by necessity personal and, if mine occasionally looks somewhat incidental, I hope it will cover essential points.

The wording of my subject suggests something usually called sociological. Being a historian and visiting a country where sociologists, social psychologists, and anthropologists are riding high and wide, I feel I have to be on my guard. Social history and sociology are not the same, though each side has to learn from the other. The historian is sometimes in danger of seeing the trees rather than the woods, while the sociologists generally see the woods, but sometimes do not know that there are different trees, or even trees at all. Or, to change over from botany to the humanities: I shall be less concerned with society as a whole or as an abstract concept than I shall be with individuals, professions, and classes. I shall not speak of inner-direction and other-direction, or similar ideas; it may be a fault in my intellectual system, but to me such concepts do not make historical sense. I shall speak of life and literature, art and craft, thought and belief, wealth and poverty. If you now feel I am an old-fashioned dodo—it just can't be helped.

There is another difference between historians and sociologists. The historian is more or less bound to stick to chronology, the sociologist is not. I repeat: more or less, for a strict rule would be deadly and make of history a timetable. I shall deal in these lectures with various historical phases. I shall not speak of a Greco-Roman civilization, which, in my view, did not exist before, say, the second century A.D. I shall concentrate on the Greek world of the centuries down to the fifth and fourth centuries B.C., and the Roman Republic—that is to say, I shall not speak of the Hellenistic Age nor of the Roman Empire.

What do we mean by the word "civilization"? There is not one clear-cut way to answer this question. We may distinguish, if we wish, between civilization and culture, though not in the way of the Germans who take *Zivilisation* as a minor, mainly technical, standard of life, and culture as the higher sort, possibly even invented by the Greeks. In English, so it seems to me, culture is usually the result of an individual's intellectual and spiritual development, and civilization a way of life, of thought, of literary and artistic achievements—a social phenomenon. There is no civilization of an individual, only of a community or society. After all, the word derives from *civis, civilis*. It emanates from an upper class, though the lower classes have a share in it. On the other hand, no civilization is possible without creative minds, and they are by necessity the minds of individual men and women. The interconnection of society and the individual is at the bottom of every civilization. Man *and* society always means man *in* society, and this is true, not only of the compliant member of society, but also of the reformer and even the revolutionary. In one way or another, they all are bound to the traditions—social, intellectual, artistic—which are being kept alive by and in the community. A community may be more or less civilized, but probably none was ever entirely uncivilized.

What indeed do we mean by "society" or "community"? These words have been used and misused in so many meanings that it is impossible to settle on any one. Moreover, they imply different things according to historical circumstances. They also imply a development from a more primitive to a more complex society; naturally, the impact of this development on the Greek mind changed accordingly. For our purpose, it will be sufficient to see society as that part of the population which, at a certain time, can be regarded as the necessary background for the creative individual. This may be a whole people or a social stratum. This background, this milieu, will, of course, never fully explain a work of art or thought, but neither will that be fully understood without some knowledge of its social and spiritual surroundings. There may be some general scheme into which our observations will fit but, if I can help it, no scheme will be imposed upon the facts.

I say facts, but we know that all historical facts are transmitted to us by a long line of tradition, down to the present speaker, a tradition in which, whether deliberately or not, facts have been selected, distorted, changed. The historian can only hope, by using methodical criticism and imagination, to disentangle, to some extent, the confused threads, and not to add too much to the inherited obscurities and uncertainties by his own work, conditioned as it will be, even in the most honest searcher for truth, by his own circumstances in time and place and surroundings.

Now we turn at last from the abstract and the general to the concrete and specific. Our chief evidence will be contemporary literature, art, and thought. These all speak to us, but probably nothing speaks more clearly than the voice of the poet; it is he who expresses, more than anybody else, the spirit of an epoch. The interpretation of our evidence will teach us something about social phenomena and forces, which may include religion as well as economics, and codes of behavior as well as individual experience. The first phase of Greek civilization—apart from its prehistoric predecessors—is the Mycenaean Age (c. 1400–1150 B.C.). We know that the Mycenaeans were Greeks, but we also know (from vast archaeological evidence) that they were deeply influenced by the earlier and highly advanced civilization of Minoan Crete. The rulers were rich, but whether mainly from war booty or from the tributes of their subjects is not known. The recently deciphered tablets in Linear B, though in their details still a very uncertain source, have provided us with a fair amount of "technical" information, using the word in its widest sense. We now know that the Mycenaean royal household was a complex bureaucratic organization of the kind common in the Ancient East. This was a monarchy, worlds away from any later Greek monarchy, including that described by Homer, and yet even this strange setting contained traces clearly pointing to the Greeks of later times. For one thing, the Mycenaean rulers lived a life very different from that of the Cretan kings. They lived in fortresses of amazing strength, far too strong for any real warfare; the palace within consisted of one or two central buildings of the primitive, very simple house type, the megaron, which I still think most likely came from the north and which later survived in the shape of the Greek temple (see fig. 1). The palace also contained a sanctuary of the chief god or goddess, whose priest the king probably was. The kings had gold and ivory, and Cretan artists worked for them. And, though the life of the Mycenaeans in general was rough and their culture under the spell of Crete, they were by no means a primitive people. Their architecture, for instance, as shown not only in their fortifications, but most impressively by their great beehive tombs (see fig. 2), was far more monumental than that of Crete, where the palaces were huge and open, with all sorts of "modern comforts," baths, water pipes, and even flushing toilets. The Mycenaeans liked war and hunting, especially in chariots; even women would drive. The Minoans had preferred a leisurely and luxurious life with performances by professional athletes, male and female (see fig. 3). In these, as well as in Minoan society generally, women played an important part. This was reflected in their religion, too, or the process may have been the other way round. The "Mother of the Animals" and the Great Mother Goddess, both known in Anatolia and Syria, were the leading ladies of the Cretan Pantheon (see fig. 6). The word "ladies" is appropriate, for these goddesses wore the same fashionable, rococolike dresses as the ladies of the court (see fig. 4), very different from the simple chiton or tunic worn by Mycenaean women. The Mycenaeans had their sky and mountain god Zeus, while Minoan goddesses survived in Artemis and Gaia, perhaps also in Athena.

The Mycenaean kings lived up to the challenges of their frightening citadels, of the art and luxury of the Minoans, of the demands of a ruthless power policy. It is possible that the Mycenaean monarchy combined traces of the Oriental priest-king and the Indo-European chieftain. It is likely that under the kings an upper class, an aristocracy, developed, which was perhaps less a courtiers' class as in Crete than a class of independent minor rulers and knights. And the people? The tablets mention a large number of professions, all kinds of craftsmen and traders, many of them royal servants, others slaves of a god or of the king. Women served in many ways, for instance, as spinners and weavers or as bath attendants. The question of land tenure is still open, though it certainly was complicated and probably based on what we may call a feudal structure of society. However, all this must remain hypothetical, for so far we see only "through a glass darkly."

In the Mycenaean Age, the Greeks, for the first though not the last time in their history, accepted and reshaped a foreign civilization to suit their own genius. The foreign element, especially in the main trends of religion and the greatest achievements in art, proved the stronger. The wonderful use, for instance, that the Minoan artists made of natural life, of plants and animals, both of land and sea, was something the Greeks did not inherit; but there can be little doubt that this first marriage between the Greeks and the East opened the way to a great future. There was soon to be a divorce, or rather a separation, but as sometimes happens, they were to remarry under changed conditions; henceforth the Oriental partner always was the weaker. But after a number of invasions, the last of which was the "Dorian" (c. 1100–1000 B.C.), through destruction and a new era of primitiveness in these centuries, the Greeks found a new unity beyond the scattered world of tribal and local communities.

The unity of the Greek mind found its expression in Homer, who probably lived in the eighth century. However different his social world was from that of the Mycenaeans, the tradition was never completely broken, and even in the arts and crafts, there was a decline and a revival rather than a sudden break. The tradition included not only sites of settlement and shapes of buildings, but also gods and forms of worship and, above all, the oral handing down of heroic poetry. One of the most interesting aspects of this was the attempts of the poet of the *Iliad* or *Odyssey* to deal with traditional material which he no longer fully understood. For instance, chariot warfare had been customary in Mycenaean times, but in Homer the chariot serves virtually only as a means of transport between tent and battlefield; fighting is done on foot, and the charioteer must keep close to the dismounted warrior. These tactics, perhaps, were never actually used.

Epic or heroic poetry, the first and perhaps greatest emanation of the Greek mind, is the work of professionals. It is true, the kings and noble knights could sing themselves about the "deeds of men," as Achilles does (*Il.* 9.186). I believe it is equally true, however, that there was finally one great poet who composed (and perhaps wrote) the *Iliad*, substantially as we have it now. Whether he is the author of the *Odyssey* as well, is part of the Homeric question which I wish to avoid as far as possible. Scholars' views differ widely, but there is little doubt about the long oral tradition before Homer. I abstain from speaking of possible ties of heroic poetry with magic songs. Neither do I believe there was once a time when only the noble heroes themselves sang the praise of great men and great events, although many knew how to sing and to play the lyre—this was part of aristocratic life. Achilles knew, and so did Patroclus, waiting to continue when his friend would stop. Odysseus "knew how to tell a story like a bard" (*Od.* 11.368), and for a whole month he told Aeolus "the story of Ilion, the ships of the Argives and the return of the Achaeans" (*Od.* 10.14f.). We must assume that he did that again "like a bard." It would have been out of place to introduce a professional singer into the tent of Achilles when his own singing was a solace in his self-imposed loneliness. But professional singers probably existed ever since sacred and epic poetry began, though it must have taken time before contemporary events turned into the myths of epic song.

The *aoidoi* or bards had a very vivid picture of the past in their minds, preserved through all kinds of variations as one generation after another heard from their youth the songs which they themselves would sing later on. Pertinent parts of the oral tradition were always in the mind of the singer, but, while singing and playing the lyre, he made up his own version. We can still see the lyre-players or their god in Minoan, Mycenaean, and post-Mycenaean pictures. These singers also played the accompaniment to ritual dances or funeral rites, when either they or a choir would sing (see fig. 5). Once they were important and cherished members of the king's household like the bard to whose care Agamemnon left his wife when he sailed against Troy (*Od.* 3.267), or Phemius at Ithaca "who sang to the suitors under compulsion" (*Od.* 1.154, etc.). From members of the royal household they might become honored men in a community such as Demodocus at Scheria (*Od.* 8.43ff., 471ff.), or they became migrants, wandering from court to court, from banquet to banquet, wherever their services were wanted. Religious festivals, often of local importance only, must have offered good opportunities for a bard's performance. The singers continued to be held in high esteem (cf. *Od.* 17.518), and to compare them to wandering beggars seems off the mark. In a well-known passage of the *Odyssey* (17.383) they are mentioned among the *demiurgi,* that is to say, among those who work for the community, though they do not belong to it. The singers were honored as experts, like the seer, the physician, and the shipbuilder. The singer as well as his song could be called *thespis,* inspired by a god; Demodocus is called *dios,* divine, because "a god has granted him his singing to delight the people whatever his mind urges him to sing" (*Od.* 8.44ff.). Apollo, and the Muses in particular, have given him his art and wisdom. They have taught him to see the world as it is, and thus to put it into song. This was even more significant when the singer was blind as was the old man from Chios (*Hymn. Hom.* 3.172). There is an essential truth in the idea of Homer as a blind man, a man who saw both the visible and the invisible in his mind.

Milton was blind when he wrote *Paradise Lost*. There was a traditional image of the singer which still prevailed when the singers had grown into a definite group of professionals who sang to an aristocratic audience. If we take together the whole development of epic poetry, the part it played in its own time as well as for posterity, it seems right to call the early age of Greek social history "the Age of the Singers."

In order to measure the importance of a civilization at a certain time, it is at least as important to know about the public as about the poets and artists. "Homeric" society has been frequently described, although the word "Homeric" hardly implies any definite period. That society contained elements different in time and therefore different in conditions. It is not possible to draw a uniform picture. Yet, in all its variety, it had an essential unity, and if there were many contrasts, they were more or less those of any society fully alive: heroism and humanity as well as ferocity and inhumanity, piety and independence, love and hatred. From our point of view it is most significant that the aristocrats who acted as patrons of the singers were a class, strictly separated from the mass of the people, bound together by kinship, by wealth, and by a code of social behavior, which was chiefly regulated by concepts of honor and shame (*aidos*) and at the same time served the solidarity of the noble class. It was a male society, but Homer never speaks of pederasty. Women played their part in the home. The public role given to Arete, Alcinous' queen, is unique; it is either part of the general Phaeacian fairy tale or a survival of an early period when matriarchy may have been the rule. Homer's society was one of self-centered individuals, where valor or excellence (*arete*) was based on material splendor, manly prowess, and generous hospitality rather than on any strictly ethical issues. It was a society which created the world of the gods in its own image, but nevertheless felt dependent on their great power and the even greater one of the dark forces ruling the fates of men *and* gods. The Olympian all-too-human society could only have been created by a people who had left the soil from which the cults and gods originally had come and who had abandoned their ancient religious and social ties; they were immigrants to Asia Minor from the motherland.

Homeric aristocracy was to undergo considerable changes before it would be able to adapt itself to new standards, when men and gods would belong to one community, when gods like Demeter and Dionysus, neglected by Homer, would be great deities again, and when even the Olympians would recover their connection with the forces of nature. By then the nobleman no longer would be a heroic individual, but a man sharing in the leadership of the Polis. It remains a source of unending wonder that Homer with his pre-Polis standards could remain *the* poet and the principal teacher of his people. We must not overstate the didactic element in Homer, though this quality has something to do with the position of the singers. Homer later became the book that everybody read, even the schoolboys. If a special explanation for this is needed, apart from the force of his poetry and his creation of ideal human prototypes, it is that the aristocratic class, through all the vicissitudes of its history, acted as a kind of guardian of epic poetry. When the performance of this poetry, as we shall see, was taken over by the rhapsodes, and Homer, as it were, became the property of the whole people, this was only possible because the nobles had maintained a leadership and an influence which was just as much cultural as political. It was a legacy that made poetry the predecessor of philosophy and the guide for Greek society.

One day, the singer was no longer called an *aoidos,* but a *rhapsodes* (see fig. 13). The Greeks thought the new word derived from *rhabdos,* meaning staff or wand, and we know indeed that later singers held a staff instead of a lyre, that is to say, they recited rather than sang. The etymology, however, is wrong, and recent attempts explain the word and related passages (Ps.-Hesiod, fr. 265; Pind., *Nem.* 2.2) by referring to the verb *rhaptein,* which means "sew together"; the rhapsode was a "stitcher of song." This may be nothing but a metaphor, perhaps derogatory, taken from the language of handicraft. But it confirms what the Greeks explained by a false etymology, that the poet was now no longer a creative artist, but simply a craftsman. The question arises as to when that change occurred.

During the late eighth century the hexameter reached its full perfection and widespread use (note the famous inscription on a Dipylon prize vase). This verse had undoubtedly undergone a considerable period of development—how long, we cannot say. Whether one could sing and not only recite hexameters is not for the historian to decide; when the lyre disappeared, the tune of the chanting must have changed, but it was still some kind of musical rendering, something between pure song and mere speech. After all, the word "rhapsodes" itself contains the concept of song.

We ask again at what period the *aoidos* turned into the rhapsode. Some scholars think it happened when it became customary to recite not only single episodes, but full-length epics. The *Iliad* was recited at the Athenian festival of the Panathenaea by a number of rhapsodes in turn, probably since the time of Peisistratus. A fourth-century historian, quoted by Diogenes Laertius (1.57), even attributed to Solon the rule that the rhapsodes should recite Homer "from a cue, so that where the first has finished, from there the second shall begin." It is unlikely that Solon gave such a rule, but the method had been in use before; we need only think of Achilles and Patroclus. It is, however, known, for instance, from Yugoslavia that long epics have been sung by one singer over a period of several weeks. Thus, the argument is inconclusive.

The island of Chios played a special part in post-Homeric development. In the Delian Hymn to Apollo (*Hymn. Hom.* 3.169) of the seventh to sixth century it is the blind man from Chios who, in a kind of self-advertisement, wants to be regarded as "the sweetest of the singers"; he was a true bard. It was also at Chios that the family of the Homerids were known as performers of epic poetry. Whether descendants of the poet of the *Iliad* or not, they were no longer true poets. They served a public need by their recitals, probably also by writing some verse, such as the additions to Hesiod or some of the Cyclic epics. There was a demand for more and more material, even without concern for artistic composition. At that moment, the personal union between poet and rhapsode had definitely come to an end.

Had it been likewise one or two centuries earlier? We have Hesiod, who belongs to the Boeotia of about 700 B.C. Each of his two poems is hardly longer than a single book of the *Iliad* and could easily have been performed in one stretch. He calls himself a bard (*aoidos*), but tells us that the Muses gave him a laurel branch (*Theog.* 30). This was a branch of Apollo's holy tree; it was at the same time a *skeptron,* a staff; he was both a poet and a rhapsode. Incidentally, he could not have spoken of himself as a rhapsode, for that word does not fit into the epic meter. Moreover, he certainly was a poet in his own right. The break between creative poetry and spoken recital had not yet occurred. In his best parts, Hesiod has a force and a personal passion which made him the forerunner of new developments in the future.

The world in which Hesiod lived was very different from that of Homer. A poet who was also a farmer, or a farmer who was also a poet, he made poems for a new audience.

The story of his "interview" (if we may call it that) with the Muses (*Erga* 1ff.) was more than a conventional allegory. In a hard and prosaic world he suddenly felt that he was not just a peasant; the gift of the Muses was to him a very real experience. Hesiod changed the contents of epic poetry. "The race of the eternal gods," as he says, is his first theme, that of the *Theogony,* the origin of the gods and, as it were, of Zeus' ascendancy. When among the catalogues of gods in the *Theogony* (75ff.) he enumerates the nine Muses, he calls Calliope "the most wonderful of them all," for she, the Muse of the beautiful voice (and here comes a surprise), helps the princes when they act as judges. The Muses are the sponsors of the poet Hesiod, but the Muse to whom he owes his voice as a singer is at once connected with one of the main themes of his poetry, judges and justice. If Hesiod did not sing of the great events of the heroic past or of those of his own times, of migration and colonization, it was because he was fully occupied with his own needs, material as well as spiritual, and his cares and worries were also those of his audience. He knew the hard life of the poor farmer who suffered from the injustice of the ruling princes, whom Hesiod calls *dorophagoi,* "gift-eating," accused them of taking bribes. He believed in divine forces, very different from the aristocratic Olympian society of Homer; his beliefs included magic and superstition (as we *and* Homer would call them), but this also meant a moral revolution which turned the gods into ethical forces and imposed ethical demands on man. Hesiod fulfilled the task which his genius had set him in a twofold way. Of his two poems, the *Theogony* was to deal with the basic theme of the origins and the genealogy of the gods; it was to become a piece of repertory among the rhapsodes. The later poem, *Works and Days* (*Erga*), was mainly concerned with his own griefs and ethical maxims, and the farmer's day-to-day work. Both poems are clearly didactic;

Hesiod may have learned something from Oriental poetry. Homer became the general teacher of his people, although the aims of the bards had been chiefly to entertain, to raise tension, tears, and laughter. Hesiod consciously regarded his task as one of instruction and education. Even mythical stories, like that of the Ages of Man, are inserted, often invented, for didactic reasons. Apart from them, the mythical world of the *Theogony*, though filled with deeper meaning, is a pedantic and yet contradictory scheme of innumerable genealogies. Hesiod accepted the task demanded by public opinion and turned away from that art of the Muses which, as he says, could tell beautiful lies—clearly an allusion to Homer. Hesiod aimed at teaching the truth.

A whole profession does not alter its traditions and methods, unless it is so compelled by circumstances. The singers no longer found their audience at the feasts of kings and noblemen. Hesiod, though very learned, spoke to the people. To Homer and his audience, the "people" hardly existed, and the gods shared such views. When Apollo for nine days sent his deadly arrows into the Greek army (*Il.* 1.43ff.), only common soldiers were hit; none of the kings died from the plague. Only after his death did Achilles realize that to be poor and a landless worker was still better than to rule over the dead (*Od.* 11.489ff.). There are two men of low rank who play an important part in Homer, Thersites and Eumaeus. They could not be more different, but their difference is not only that of free and slave, nor is either of them depicted as a representative of a class. Thersites was beaten, an occasion for laughter for the army; nobody, not even the suitors, would ever have dared to beat Eumaeus. But neither for the humiliation of the free soldier nor for the lack of freedom of the swineherd does the poet show any real understanding; one is a malicious caricature, the other an idealized portrait, but both remain within the sphere of an exclusive and patriarchal society. In many of Homer's similes, on the other hand, the heroic Homeric sphere is replaced by scenes of human life, of the craftman's work and even the events of the kitchen. By then, the exclusive aristocratic world had changed. Hesiod was the first to sing of the people as they were, to whom he belonged himself. In such surroundings, at the larger gatherings of townsfolk or peasants there must have arisen an urge to listen to a singer. It was then that both Homer and Hesiod began to play the part, described by Herodotus (2.53), of those who created for the Greeks the world of their gods. Ever after, poets were regarded in Greece—whether or not they themselves intended it—as teachers and preachers. We shall return to this aspect.

It has become more or less the accepted view that Homer and Hesiod together are proof of the greatness of the eighth century. Yet, in a sense, they were not contemporaries. Exact dating is impossible, but the geographical distance between Asia Minor and Boeotia caused such a difference in social climate that it is difficult to take the two poets, in spite of their obvious interconnection, as an expression of the same age. Hesiod is, at any rate, the younger poet who has learnt from Homer, and although husbandry is eternal, Hesiod's social world too belongs to a later phase. Homer's kings were, at the same time, farmers who might work the soil while their sons, perhaps, tended the herds. But Homer's was an affluent society. Work there is, but it is pleasant; think of Odysseus' "joy in carpentry" in building his marital bed. Much is said of leisure and feasting. Hesiod's farmer has also some leisure, but only in winter, and even then there is plenty of work in the house and the barn. The difference is more than that between rich and poor.

Hesiod's two poems are remarkably different in content as well as in personal attitude. There is unmistakably the same mind at work, above all the same religious attitude, but from the *Theogony* to the *Erga,* Hesiod's personal relation to his rulers has changed. Those "princes" who in the *Theogony* are descendants of Zeus, giving right judgments in the Agora, revered men of wisdom and justice, play a very different part in the *Erga.* In between, Hesiod had his legal fight with his brother whom he accused of having gained the paternal property by bribing the judges. He suffered personal injustice; he could not get a just verdict from the nobles, the human judges; and thus he became the passionate prophet of divine justice. He had claimed that the *aoidos,* "singing the deeds of earlier men and praising the immortals" (*Theog.* 98ff.), could relieve a man from his sorrows; now he used his own power of song to admonish his weak brother and to proclaim right against wrong. The hawk—in that fable which Hesiod told the unjust princes—might kill the nightingale, although, as he wrote with delightful self-irony, she was an *aoidos,* but, in the end, Justice, Dike—by the will of her father Zeus—would conquer. The claims and the rights of the lower classes—here the poor Boeotian farmers—became the clarion call which fully inaugurated the citizens' community. The passionate refusal of injustice by the individual was at the same time a social problem, the problem of the Polis. Solon, a century later, learned from Hesiod, and, in trying to help the oppressed and enslaved, took the decisive step toward practical social statesmanship.

As a poet Hesiod had no successor of any standing. Epic poetry was on its last legs. Also in his new subject—farming—he found no successor until the time of the Romans. A man who was a great character, though as a poet not a genius, was for centuries the only poet to speak of the daily work of the farmer. His description, though incoherent and selective, is most impressive. Compared with Homer, it shows the other end of the social scale; it displays at the same time a new code of behavior, that of an honest, hard-working, parsimonious and pious, even superstitious peasant, a good neighbor and, to some extent, a family man. He hates the sea, but he loves the soil, the plants, the animals; above all, as a farmer, he is a craftsman who knows all about the "works of Demeter" (*Erga* 393). Agriculture was at all times and in practically every Greek state the basis of the economy, and the work of the peasant, however hard, remained honored. Hesiod had written on both its moral foundations and its day-to-day practice. When we admire the great poets and artists of classical Greece, who all felt themselves Homer's disciples, we should not forget the poet who spoke for the ordinary man. If the main theme of modern literature is "love," Homer's chief subject was "war and adventure," and Hesiod's "work." Moreover, Hesiod was the first poet to conceive the idea of Zeus as the guardian of supreme justice, an idea which was to guide Greek religious and philosophical thought for all time to come. This idea colored the religion of the community as well, and it was the basis of the claim of the Polis to be the bearer of justice, the state under Dike and the Law, a claim which was to be supported by the written legislation of individual lawgivers.

The process we have been describing would not have been possible without the invention of the alphabet. Greeks who also knew Phoenician, perhaps at a trading settlement on the Syrian coast, adapted the Semitic alphabet to the Greek language, probably in the early eighth century. It makes little difference, in my opinion, whether Homer, out of the oral tradition, dictated or wrote his composition (as certainly did Hesiod), or whether that was done by another man of the same period. During the later eighth century the art of writing spread widely, though naturally our evidence is scanty. The Greek alphabet developed into several regional forms, but essentially it was one important bond to make the

Greek people conscious of their unity; less strong a bond, however, than common language, the gods, and the Homeric legacy. The art of writing did not mean the end of creative epic poetry, though it was the beginning of the end. The oral tradition can be traced everywhere, but it had begun to die out. The transition from the bards to the rhapsodes did not simply coincide with the appearance of written poetry. The process took its time, as in the social field. The eighth and seventh centuries saw the rise of a new class and the foundation of new communities. The same period saw the new weapons and new tactics of the hoplites, and they were the citizens who demanded their rightful place in society and state. The emergence of the Polis provided a new framework for poetry and poets. In this transitional period epic art became a craft, but the change was not uniform. Among the so-called Homeric hymns, which are longer or shorter poems in hexameters dedicated to various deities, some are routine work, used probably by rhapsodes as the introduction to an epic story; others, however, are very beautiful poems indeed, recited at special festivals of Apollo or of Aphrodite or Hermes. They prove that even in this period, which lasted into the sixth century, there were a few great poets who adapted the epic tradition to a changing world.

A similar, though not identical, situation existed in vase painting, which for many centuries was a major art reflecting the main trends of the Greek mind. We know today that Athens had a leading position in the period of protogeometric and geometric styles, from the tenth to the eighth century, and that the art of the period was remarkable, even sophisticated. This has been a somewhat surprising discovery, partly with regard to the position of Athens, and partly in the estimation of that art. For a long time, it was felt that there was a strong contrast between the high perfection of Homer's poetry and the "primitive" art of the geometric style. Recently, the pendulum has swung to the other extreme. Today we are acquainted with abstract art and, therefore, better equipped than earlier generations to value the work of that early period, and to realize that it was a new and high form of art, even though it originated in a time of new and genuine primitiveness.

In our context it is relevant to ask for whom the potters and painters worked. Many of the vases are so large and show such a display of ornamental and figurative decoration that they must have been very expensive. Most of them, the "Dipylon Vases," were found in the Kerameikos cemetery at Athens and served the wealthy at funerals and for the worship of the dead (see figs. 8, 9, 11). Besides, cups and jugs were for show rather than for practical use, or, if for use, they were for a rich man's table. The pictures on the geometric vases of the eighth century, apart from ornaments and animal friezes, represent religious dances, large and solemn funerals, battles and ships, chariot races, and men fighting a centaur or lion. The sphinxes and griffins of the Minoan as well as the later proto-Corinthian periods are absent, but that does not prove that the pictures were, as at least one leading archaeologist has maintained, "scenes of everyday life." One example may suffice. Throughout vase painting lions were a symbol of savage strength. They were unknown in Greece, though perhaps not in Asia Minor, and Homer mentions them countless times in his similes. And there are other reasons for believing that we are allowed to draw a more general conclusion: most of the scenes on the vases are likely to have been taken from heroic stories; the vase owners surely enjoyed them as much as they liked listening to a bard.

We know little of Athenian life during the ninth and eighth centuries. There was a changeover from monarchy to the rule of an aristocracy. At first this probably consisted of no more than a few families, who at an early stage may have been called *eupatridai*—the "sons of noble fathers." We have noticed that they were wealthy; for other details we must look to the vases. A frequent feature of the vases is the ships which are variations of one type, a warship with a ram (figs. 9, 10). Had Athens a navy in the eighth century? There were naval actions by Athens in the later seventh century: wars for Salamis and for Sigeum, but, as far as we know, the fighting was only done on land. Still, the troops had to be transported. Further evidence is the institution of the forty-eight *naukrariai,* based on the same number of captains (*naukraroi*) and thus of forty-eight ships. It is unlikely that this organization, first personal, then local, was older than the seventh century, perhaps the late eighth, but it may have had some predecessors. Did the painters copy ships at Phaleron? It is possible. But it is also possible that (as in the case of the lions) they worked from a traditional prototype. There are scenes of a battle for or near the ships (see fig. 9), and it is difficult not to think of the *Iliad*. The shield of the warriors on the Dipylon vases—shaped like a double axe and quite unsuitable as a body cover (see figs. 8, 11)—could probably be explained as a distorted memory of the figure-8-shaped Minoan shield, a mixture of reality, tradition, and imagination; in the same way the type of ship might easily originate from the eighth century's conception of what was "heroic." The ship scenes each clearly tell a story; that was of greater interest to the painters than the nautical details which they sometimes seem to have misunderstood. It is a similar phenomenon that none of the vases, as far as I know, shows a contemporary warrior, a hoplite—or had Athens not yet hoplite soldiers at that time?

Pottery can tell us a little about the upper class for whom the craftsmen worked. The figure scenes might sometimes depict a funeral or a chariot race as they were known among the nobles. But we may doubt whether even they quite fit into the Athenian scene; it would be understandable if the painters tried to raise the contemporary occasion to a heroic level. Battle scenes from Troy, Heracles killing the Nemean lion or strangling the Stymphalian birds, the *Aktorione-Moleone,* the twins fighting in one body (*Il.* 11.709) (see fig. 7), the shipwreck of Odysseus (see fig. 10)—these are the subjects we can most likely discern on the vases. Ever since that time, mythology, the fruit of epic poetry, remained the favorite theme of vase painting, and the citizen society followed later in the steps of their noble predecessors.

The prominence of Athens at that time can to some extent be explained by the fact that it was, on the mainland, the only Mycenaean state of importance not invaded and destroyed by the Dorians. It is quite possible that a good many fugitives from other parts of Greece found a refuge in Athens. Archaeology and mythology confirm—against earlier doubts—Thucydides' statement (1.2.6) that Athens, though a country with poor soil, had grown in population through the arrival of newcomers, a state of affairs which led to the Ionian migration to Asia Minor. Moreover, for more than two centuries the dead at Athens were cremated and not buried. A full explanation of this remarkable fact and of the return to burial in the eighth century has not yet been found. It seems to the point, though hardly sufficient as a full explanation, to assume that Attica was temporarily overpopulated. However, both forms of removing the dead were very old, and sometimes could exist side by side in the same period. There was perhaps less change than is often assumed in people's thoughts on death and afterlife when they replaced one form by the other, though religious beliefs must have played a part. At Athens, noble families, in particular, who in the ninth century had had their own cemetery, had accepted cremation. It seems there were different strata of society, perhaps even of different origin, who followed different religious rituals. In that period of migration inside Greece and emigration to the east, a good many people passed through Athens, and some, perhaps many, would have stayed on.

It is not possible to say much about the social standing of the potters and painters. During the eighth century they reached a high standard of art and technique, aiming at a wholly admirable harmony of shape and proportion. The painters knew many heroic stories, most likely from listening to singers or rhapsodes, or by the usual transmission from parents to children; it is just possible that they may have read Homer. They were not uneducated nor a suppressed class; perhaps they approached as craftsmen a status similar to that of the professional rhapsodes. I remind you of the two lines in Hesiod (*Erga* 25f.) when he speaks of the good Eris ("strife"): "and potter is angry with potter, and builder with builder, and beggar is jealous of beggar, and singer of singer." Athenian pottery spread all over Greece and the Aegean; there must have been a good deal of trading, and it is likely that at least from the late eighth century onward the Athenians themselves did some trading, though among the ships pictured there is none that could be called a cargo boat.

The vases may tell us heroic stories, but they do not tell us anything about the change from the bards to the rhapsodes. Nor, in fact, can I accept the view that the shift of outlook from the *Iliad* to the *Odyssey* is reflected in Athenian vase painting. On the other hand, the decline of the geometric style, which gave way to the monsters and colorful ornaments of the orientalizing style and for a time let Athenian pottery play second fiddle, coincided with the change in social structure and the inner unrest which characterized the seventh century and the Archaic Age as a whole.

# II. The Archaic Age

According to one modern scholar, "The World of Hesiod" was followed by "The Lyric Age." In this view the eighth century belongs on the whole to the preceding era, and the seventh and sixth centuries are regarded as a unit. It is, however, essential to realize that the eighth century is an end as well as a beginning. The "Lyric Age" may be a fitting successor to the "Age of the Singers"; but the latter is confined to the "heroic" age whose society as a whole is expressed by that title, while the former covers only one side, however important, of a period which was also the age of colonization, of tyrants and lawgivers, of Spartan consolidation and Athenian reforms—the age also of the first philosophers and the growth of the mystery religions. Lyric poetry, moreover, lived on into the fifth century, with poets as great as Simonides, Pindar, and Bacchylides. It is, on the other hand, true that the larger part of our literary evidence for the seventh and sixth centuries derives from lyric poetry. Greek literature, in fact, in its essential outlines, developed, as has already been seen by Nietzsche almost a century ago, from epic to lyric, from lyric to tragedy, from tragedy to prose, thus displaying the various branches of literature not so much side by side as one after another, though with a good deal of overlapping. If this scheme were our general historical guide, classical Greece would become "The Tragic Age," and curiously enough, as we shall see, this title would not be inappropriate; again it was Nietzsche who in 1873 wrote about "Philosophy in the Tragic Age of Greece." Still, the usual name for the eighth to sixth centuries is

"archaic"; it was probably first used by archaeologists, and
it means regarding the period simply as the age preceding
the classical age, which seems an unsatisfactory reason, for
the period had very great importance of its own. It witnessed, above all, the awakening of the individual and its
rise within the Polis. I must, however, admit that I know
of no other suitable name, and therefore shall retain the
word "archaic" as a convenient, purely chronological symbol.

The Archaic Age has also been called a revolution or, on
the other hand, a Greek Renaissance. The latter expression
seems particularly inept. What was reborn? Mycenaean
Greece? Certainly not, and yet the intended meaning can
only be that a new civilization arose after the "Dark Ages."
Even Eduard Meyer has spoken of the Greek Middle Ages,
but the analogies to medieval times and the Renaissance are
misleading, even thoroughly wrong. We have seen how the
period of the "Dark Ages" meant in fact a new beginning;
the Archaic Age grew out of that beginning. It is more important to ask whether there was a revolution. There can
be no doubt that at the end of the archaic period things
looked very different indeed from what they had been
before. Political structure, social conditions, intellectual
atmosphere, literature, and art—all had undergone a great
change. Yet there was never a sudden break, and after all
that is a *conditio sine qua non* when we speak of a revolution. I shall try to depict the age in its essential aspects, but
I realize that is not an easy task. The Archaic Age is two
and one half millennia away from us, and with our frag-
mentary evidence we know perhaps even less about it than
about the Homeric world. It is a very complex age, and it
will not be possible to follow a purely chronological line.

To Homer, the non-Greek world had been fairy-tale
country, to Hesiod it was unknown and of no interest; it
was beyond reach behind the barriers of the sea. To the
Greeks of the archaic period it was a field for colonization,

for adventure, for mercenary service, for trade, for increased knowledge, for gaining a higher cultural level. Many people who left their cities were driven from their homes by poverty and oppression, others were aristocrats like Sappho's brother who sold his wine at Naucratis in Egypt and fell in love there with a beautiful hetaera, or Alcaeus' brother who served in the army of Nebuchadnezzar. Solon was a nobleman trading abroad. Second and third sons who had no claim to the family estate, must have been among the colonists and traders, and the creation of new landed gentries in most of the colonies confirms the large share of the aristocracy. Trade and colonization did not always go hand in hand. The majority of those who settled abroad came because of land hunger; many of them were impoverished peasants, and even among the traders and those who built up new manufactures many were from the lower classes. Our knowledge is scanty, but it seems evident that the great expansion during the seventh and sixth centuries was the work of all strata of society, though the aristocrats provided the leadership. It is also important to realize that the colonists included men from almost all parts of Greece and the Aegean. This universality and the guidance in the later phase given by the priests of Delphi are probably the chief reasons for the fantastic success of the spread of Greek communities over most of the shores of the Mediterranean. The Greeks had frequently to struggle with the natives; they found conditions sometimes favorable and sometimes not; but, supported by the growing prosperity of the motherland and Ionia, they created a Hellas beyond the seas, a Hellas even greater than *Magna Graecia,* the flourishing Greek cities of Italy. Despite the political isolation of each colony, despite differences in character and growth, despite rivalries and fights, there was everywhere one and the same Greek civilization, the civilization of the whole Greek people.

The colonization may have prevented revolutions at some

places; in others the social situation led to the rise of political individuals, the tyrants or lawgivers, of whom we have to say more. Domestic strife (which the Greeks called *stasis*) frequently occurred, wars were fought and even, as in the Lelantian War, war coalitions were formed. But the decisive line of events was different. The gradual rise of the lower classes went hand in hand with a steady rise in individual freedom and in cultural achievements. Noble descent and noble ways of life still prevailed; if Archilochus was the bastard son of a nobleman, Sappho and Alcaeus, Tyrtaeus and Theognis—even most of the early philosophers and, of course, most of the monarchic rulers who so often turned against their fellow-noblemen—all belonged to the aristocracy, although occasionally later legend obscured this fact. The voice that reaches us is that of the poets. With their passionate fervor and unbridled frankness, each in his or her own way, they displayed to the full that personal self-expression that meant the birth of lyric poetry. They and their social background cannot be understood unless we realize the erotic atmosphere which, as a rule, was bisexual, but more definitely homosexual than heterosexual. This very significant feature of Greek civilization had been practically excluded in Homer and in Hesiod, and even in Archilochus. In Hesiod we find for the first time a woman hater, although he realized that a farmer had need of a wife. Misogyny became a widespread phenomenon, and it seems inevitable to regard it as a result of what is often called "Greek love," the love between men and boys. Still, misogyny was confined to wives; the mistress of the house, honored as such, became an instrument only for the production of legitimate sons and for looking after house and property. Love poems were not dedicated to one's sweetheart; men's erotic feelings, as far as they are expressed in literature or art, belonged either to the hetaerae who knew how to make

music and how to make love, or above all to boys. The
great mass of the evidence, from the lyric poets down to
the sublimity of Socrates' Eros, is concerned with homosexual love. To it we owe the most beautiful Greek love
poems, to it the many lovely vases which by an inscribed
*kalos* celebrate the youthful charm of a noble boy. I must
ask you to forget your ideas of present-day society. In a
society in which men and women lived more or less separate
lives, it is impossible to treat this Greek love as an unnatural
vice. Derived perhaps from an earlier stage of military life
and therefore of particular strength in military Sparta,
pederasty came naturally to the Greeks. In a sense it is justifiable to say that it was a sign of health rather than of
degeneration (the latter it is today—or something of purely
individual concern). We have neither the right to condemn
it, nor indeed to take it as a model for present licentiousness.
We can only try to understand it in its own surroundings
and conditions. Just like heterosexual love, it could deterio-
rate into crude physical sensuality, but generally the relation between man and boy proved an expression of genuine
love, and a means of educating the young and promoting
noble ambitions and military heroism. Society actually accepted it as the higher form of sexual love, and pedagogy
was largely pederasty. It was, however, mainly confined to
the upper class, the ancient military class: in democratic
Athens, although it survived as shown by vase paintings
(see fig. 14) and anecdotal evidence alike, the bourgeoisie
of the fifth and fourth centuries strongly disparaged pederasty. They regarded it as typically oligarchic and Laconian.
Aristophanes' *Lysistrata* would have been impossible if most
of the Athenians had been pederasts!

So far we have emphasized the great part played by the
aristocracy in all matters of culture during the archaic
period. As the ruling and wealthy class, the nobles, even

sometimes *malgré eux,* were setting general standards, but they also frequently had to fight for their lives or at least their power. The monarchs of the period, who were called tyrants but were not such in our sense of the word, naturally favored the lower classes whose support they needed, and were hostile to the established nobility; they were foremost in upsetting the social structure, while at the same time promoting poetry and music, art and architecture. Of similar significance was the rise of a middle class, merchants grown rich, some of them noblemen, but most coming from the common townsfolk—such as the owners of larger workshops. If I now and later speak of a middle class I mean those between the nobility and the peasantry; there was no middle class in our sense of the word. The wealthy, who were not tied to a family estate, became part of the upper classes, and—in an age in which coined money had just started to influence economic life—they could sometimes even oust the nobles from political and social leadership. Finally, the ordinary peasants, free but poor, entered the political and cultural scenes and fostered traditions largely forgotten by nobility and townsfolk of which we shall hear more. Law codification secured the legal position of the non-nobles, and soon the decisive step was taken to distinguish between intentional and unintentional action, between murder and manslaughter, and thus to recognize personal responsibility.

Greek civilization at that period was many-faceted because of its many centers, differing in their structures. Prosperity through trade and manufacture helped a great deal to promote culture, but, for instance, in Chios, according to Theopompus (*FGrH* 115 F 122), export trade caused large imports of barbarian slaves. A state that early displayed democratic features but later became oligarchic was notorious for the numbers of its slaves; in fact, it was one of the rare examples in the Greek world of a society mainly based on slavery. As a cultural center Chios was not unimportant, though in no way leading. It was different with Corinth, a flourishing city under the stimulating leadership of the Cypselids. Cypselus had overthrown the aristocratic rule of the Bacchiads, and like his son Periander (and like other tyrants) brought prosperity and new cultural life to his city. Here the first stone temple was erected, the trireme invented, the first Greek coins were issued. Artisans and artists were highly valued, and Corinthian pottery was for a time leading in the Greek world. The landed gentry suffered and agriculture declined; eventually Periander's reign ended in cruelty and terror. As so often, the story of tyranny shows female or pederastic intrigues, the embittered hatred of the noble class, the people's insistence on their rights. The rule of the tyrants remained an interlude everywhere, but it left its mark on the political and social structure as well as on art and literature. The rise of the political individual, as exemplified by the tyrants, released new creative forces in all spheres of life.

The social changes would not have been so effective if the ruling nobility had not lost, by the rise of strong individuals, some of its firm and traditional coherence within its own ranks. Man, in order to gain full self-expression, had to loosen traditional bonds. The community, in the form of the clan, the social class, the group of common worship, or the Polis, was still the stronger force; but poets ceased to remain anonymous and began to write personal poetry, political leaders rose to monarchical power, individuals changed the face of society. Archilochus, about the middle of the seventh century, was the first to write exclusively about himself, his loves and hatreds, his successes and failures. His life was that of an adventurous soldier. He could not write epic poetry. We understand that he introduced

short songs in largely new meters and with a new kind of
music, serving the feelings and events of the moment. A
new realism fills the lines of his poetry, and it easily turns
against conventional concepts, even high ideals.

The son of a nobleman from Paros and a Thracian slave
girl, Archilochus despises the dandy officers, well shaved
and groomed as they strut about; he prefers the bandy-
legged short man who has his heart in the right place
(fr. 60 D). He is pouring out his own feelings, regardless
of the claims of society. He does not aim, so he tells us, at
riches or political power, but he is a terrible hater, whether
from despised love or broken friendship. A single line
(fr. 52 D) seems to reflect his fundamental social problem:
"O you poor (or: outcast) citizens, you understand my
words." The individual becomes a social voice. He no longer
acknowledges the traditional code of honor: when he loses
his shield in battle, he is happy to have saved his life and
grateful to the gods; it will be easy to get another shield
(fr. 6 D). Here, not only the facts speak but also a proud
defiance of the standards of aristocratic society. When the
same happened almost a century later to Alcaeus of Lesbos
it was no longer the same. Archilochus, with obvious self-
irony, tells us that now a Thracian would proudly use his
shield. Alcaeus turns the loss of his armor into a kind of
frivolous self-aggrandizement when he boasts that the victorious Athenians had hung his weapons up in Athena's
temple at Sigeum (fr. 428 L-P, 49a D). He was not a rebel
against society; he belonged to those upper class *hetairoi*
(fr. 129, 16 L-P) who frequently took part in *symposia,* for
which Alcaeus wrote drinking songs. He also had his share
in the fights for political power against a tyrant or among
the nobles themselves; his political friendship with Pittacus
turned into hatred when Pittacus became the master of the
city. Alcaeus' lively description of a ship tossed about by

waves and winds (fr. 73 L-P, 46 D, *cf.* 6 L-P, 119–122 D)
clearly points to the political situation of his party and the
state; as Archilochus (fr. 56 D) had used the same image
for war, thus Alcaeus anticipated the later commonplace
of the "Ship of State." While Archilochus was a fighting
man who hardly knew what he was fighting for, with
Alcaeus the lyric Muse became political.

The same can be said of the elegists. Epic tradition still
determined the language and meter of poets who wrote in
elegiac distichs, hexameter and pentameter. Callinus and
Tyrtaeus, about the middle of the seventh century, the one
in aristocratic Ionia, the other in equally exclusive Sparta,
admonished the young to fight, and if necessary to die, for
state and family, for parents and children, that is to say, for
their noble traditions. This to some extent is an eternal
theme; it had entered Greek poetry with Hector's praise
of the defense of one's fatherland (*Il.* 12.243). Tyrtaeus
(fr. 9.15 D) transmutes another word of Hector (*Il.* 3.50)
about Paris as the great evil, when he speaks of the soldier
in the front line as a "common good" "to the Polis and the
whole demos." This is the voice of the new Sparta, with
her rigid subordination of the individual citizen in the interest of state and people. However, love for one's country
and the duty to stand firm in the citizens' phalanx, became
with Tyrtaeus an urgent personal appeal, a reaction at the
same time to a period of military decline and the lack of
fighting spirit among the younger generation. Tyrtaeus
went even further; he realized how hard the Spartan yoke
was under which the Messenians suffered, but he is a Spartan, and he wishes his own people to remain masters. The
danger of the Messenian revolt was great indeed. Nothing
could be worse than the fall of the Spartans from power
and wealth. Tyrtaeus paints in the darkest colors the picture
of the man who has lost his estate and, with his family,

must go begging far from his Polis. Hateful will he be to those whom he meets as a poor man, and a shame to his noble clan (fr. 6.3ff. D).

What in Tyrtaeus is only a possibility, is fully present in other poets: the struggle of the aristocracy for its survival. Alcaeus, above all, shows the disunity of the nobles, and the danger of a one-man rule. He was for some time an exile, as was even Sappho. Details of her case are unknown, and even in Alcaeus' struggle, unimportant. What matters is the general atmosphere—even the woman with her esoteric female circle and her personal world of passion and tenderness was drawn into the restless world of her contemporaries. At the same time, it has been rightly stressed that even the most independent mind, even Archilochus, felt the loneliness and human weakness that asked for a higher power to establish a general law for all men. The ruthlessness of a soldier like Archilochus or of a partisan such as Alcaeus cried out for the restoration of divine law. And the gods were still there.

This is nowhere more manifest than with Sappho. Her intense relation with Aphrodite is not that of a priestess with a goddess, but of a mortal woman with a divine woman, under whose protection Sappho's girl pupils learned to live, to play music, and to enjoy poetry. To understand the whole phenomenon, we must again think of that society as entirely different from our own. Modern verdicts on Sappho run from "headmistress of a girls' school" to "profligate and perverse genius." All that is nonsense, although a genius she was. We cannot deny the eroticism, but we can and must strongly refute the implications of the modern use of the word "Lesbian." If anything, the feelings cultivated in Sappho's circle were bisexual. Sappho was married and had a daughter; most of her girls went away to get married, and Sappho wrote wedding songs for them. Yet, the atmosphere of her school was one of all-pervading love, and she gives a passionate description of the very malady, physical malady, of her love that brings her near death (fr. 31 L-P, 2 D); that poem could be turned by Catullus (51) into one of his poems to Lesbia. Love also meant education. It seems certain that Sappho set a high standard of civilized life; an uneducated woman who had no part in the life of Sappho's circle was despised; she will, we are told, not be remembered after death (fr. 55 L-P, 58 D, cf. 147 L-P, 59 D)—proof of an astonishing claim not only for herself, but also for her pupils. Sappho also discovered the unity of nature and personal feelings, never more movingly than in the few lines (fr. 94 D): "Set are the moon and the Pleiads; it is midnight, and time passes by. Yet I lie down alone." The simplicity of these lines and some linguistic peculiarities have caused some scholars to contest Sappho's authorship and to call them a folk song; but there are other lines which display similar feelings, and the poem is worthy of the greatest poet. Sappho was able closely to observe her own passions; her verse have a beauty and a melodious sweetness quite unique. Alcaeus, who knew her personally, paid her a tribute of reverence and admiration. She belonged to the aristocracy, and so did her pupils; the part played by them shows that at Lesbos and in nearby Lydia, from where several of the girls came, women had a remarkably high status, both inside the house and outside. The tradition of the women of the Odyssey still lingered on; Nausicaa would have fitted well into Sappho's circle. I do not pretend to have fully explained this unique phenomenon, but I hope at least that its uniqueness has been made clear.

Relations between poet and community, and thus between poetry and religion, were by necessity closer when the poet wrote choral songs. There was a very old tradition of choral singing as a part of religious rituals. Outstanding is Alcman, who probably lived through most of the seventh century, and thus was a contemporary of Tyrtaeus and slightly earlier than the poets from Lesbos. He wrote above all *Parthenia* for the ritual songs and dances of noble Spartan girl choirs. He may speak of himself when he says: "He was not a peasant nor among the learned (?) nor of Thessalian descent nor a shepherd, but he came from lofty Sardes" (fr. 16 P, 13 D). Thus, perhaps an Ionian Greek, he wrote poetry in the Laconian dialect and shared the life, the food, and the mentality of a society that at his time was highly civilized, quite different from the Sparta of a century later. In the only longer poem which has been preserved (at least in large parts), though it is difficult to understand, the girls of the choir, rivaling with another choir, form a team, held together by common training and common worship, by their pride as a group, and above all by the love and admiration they feel for their leaders. The poet depicts their joyful happiness and also the close interchange between himself and the choir. "As many girls we are, we praise the lyre player" (fr. 38 P, 20 D). The poet has entered to an astonishing degree into the feelings of the girls, but there is at the same time an unmistakable atmosphere of mutual love among them, not so very different from Sappho's group of maidens; she too had another "school" as a rival. The Spartan girls belong to the class of noble Spartiates, and they would seem actually related, "cousins" as the text indicates. It is possible that each choir was representative of a few prominent families who would be connected by marriage.

Alcman's poems, often down-to-earth and hearty, often highly poetical and spirited, reflect a Spartan life otherwise almost unknown to us. He enjoys good food and drink, but knows that in spring, before the new harvest, one has not enough to eat (fr. 20 P, 56 D); he has certain bourgeois qualities that are similarly manifest in some of the contemporary Ionian poets such as Semonides (with his lengthy and

stupid satire on women) and Mimnermus, the latter socially
as well as poetically on a fairly high level; he sings a good
deal of love, sensual love, the object of which were girls of
light virtue, and he regards old age merely as misery and
evil. Alcman, a greater poet and more independent, thinks of
himself as a member of the Damos, the whole body of
Spartan citizens, which at that time began to come forward
against the ruling oligarchy. Alcman is not a political poet
nor indeed a warrior: "a rival to the iron is the beautiful
playing of the lyre" (fr. 41 P, 100 D). The background of
his poetry is a Sparta that went with the times, that knew
wealth, culture, and beauty. In that period the production of
beautiful vases in Laconia was begun; sometimes they displayed mythological scenes, but more frequently scenes from
life, culminating in a picture like the one in which two
warriors carry a dead man (see fig. 16), or the famous
Arcesilas vase on which the king of Cyrene (and Cyrene
was an indirect colony of Sparta) is depicted supervising the
loading of a cargo ship (see fig. 15). It was in Sparta of all
places that the famous slogan of the period was coined:
*chremat' aner,* "property makes a man" (Alcaeus, fr. 360
L-P, 101 D). Trade and manufacture played their part,
though it is unlikely that even then the Spartiates had a share
in them. They loved music and poetry, they enjoyed a life
perhaps not luxurious, but easy and happy, until the emer-
gency of the Second Messenian War about the middle of the
seventh century started a social revolution which was to bring
back their traditional militarism, as preached by Tyrtaeus.
The so-called Lycurgan order slowly stifled most cultural
activities and made of Sparta from the second half of the
sixth century a military camp and an authoritarian state.

During the sixth century lyric poetry, in general, began
to decline, though it still found new themes and new ways
of expression. The patronage of tyrants and other wealthy

men became important. There was Stesichorus, the great mythologist from Sicily, whose stories displayed many bold new features; they may be reflected in the wealth of mythological vase paintings and sculptures like that "mythical anthology" of the François vase (fig. 12), or in works we know only from literary descriptions such as the Chest of Cypselus or the Amyclaean throne. As never before, myth became the playground of poetry and art. It was most likely Stesichorus who made Agamemnon a Spartan king, thus putting the leadership of Sparta far back into early times. There was Ibycus who wrote mythological stories partly to turn them into the praise of Polycrates (perhaps when the ruler of Samos still was a boy—fr. 282 P, 3 D), and other boy beauties. His love poetry reflects the life at a tyrant's court; it shows an air of artificial extravagance. There were also the light, often witty songs of love and wine by Anacreon; he too stayed at the court of Polycrates. He later went to Athens where he found a new patron in Peisistratus' son Hipparchus and after his murder a friend in Xanthippus, the father of Pericles. Like the singers of Homeric times, the poets were again the guarantors of the fame, even the immortality, of their social superiors. In their different ways, the choral songs of Ibycus and the monodies of Anacreon confirm the cultural atmosphere of the tyrants' courts. These were also partly responsible for the final flowering of lyric poetry in the fifth century, in Simonides and Pindar. There were other factors as well: the growing importance of the athletic competitions, the new patriotism of the times of the Persian wars, above all, the deepened sense of human dependency, and of divine power and justice.

Much earlier, however, elegiac poetry had become the servant of politics, a useful instrument in the struggle for social change. Taking the place of literary prose that had not yet been invented, it was used, as we saw, by Tyrtaeus

and more personally by Solon of Athens after 600 B.C. He was
a wise and just man and a courageous statesman, who in his
elegies tried to prepare for his reforms, and later to defend
them. We shall have more to say of him in the next lecture.
A younger poet of elegies was Theognis of Megara, who in
his verse expressed the deep resentment of an impoverished
nobleman against the rise of the non-nobles. Theognis (as
far as we can separate him from the vast amount of later
Theognidea) tries to teach a beloved boy, Cyrnus, the wisdom and the way of life of his aristocratic forefathers. Bitter
experience and hatred of the upstarts are mixed-up with
sensible rules of moral behavior and purely utilitarian advice.
Wine and good company play their part, also a genuine, if
narrow, patriotism. The picture that emerges is typical of a
class that has learned a doubtful wisdom in the losing civil
struggle.

Sparta and Corinth for a time were the cultural centers
in Greece, but it was on the periphery, in Ionia, Aeolia, and
the west, that the great thoughts were thought, the most
impressive temples were built, the first marble statues erected.
In the motherland, Corinth was leading in vase painting, and
then rather suddenly Athens took over. But before we speak
in the next lecture of Athens, we must speak of Miletus,
where the urge for individual freedom and self-expression
found a new field in the philosophy and natural science of
Thales, Anaximander, and Anaximenes. Apart from one
quotation from Anaximander, we know of their thoughts
and lives by later sources only, and little of that is certain;
but we are not concerned with the details of their philosophy,
their cosmology, their meteorology, rather with the fact of
their sudden appearance. Is it possible to find an explanation
why at Miletus in the sixth century individuals lived who
discovered the principles of future science and philosophy?
It may have some significance that, as far as we know, these

philosophers were at the same time aristocrats, political leaders, and practical men of the world. Herodotus (1.170) tells us that Thales was the first to draw up a plan for uniting the Ionian cities; Anaximander founded a Milesian colony on the Black Sea (Aelian, *VH* 3.17). They were known for various mathematical and technical devices, they traveled a good deal. Anaximander drew a map of the known world, and Thales predicted an eclipse of the sun. In most of these matters they had learnt from Babylon or Egypt. Miletus with her flourishing trade, her connections with the East, and her colony Naucratis in the Nile delta, was a place where the conflux of goods caused one of ideas as well. Moreover, the Ionian mind always tended to be rational, and in that period the Greek mind generally was to outgrow the stage of mythological cosmogony. The decisive step was to ask what was the *arche* of things, and that meant origin as well as principle; the world no longer started from divine persons and actions. Myth was replaced, if only partially, by reason. Anaximander's extant fragment leads beyond that, though it is difficult, if not impossible, to understand its full meaning. When he says that the existing things "pay penalty and retribution to each other for their injustice, according to the order of time," he introduces the concepts of right and wrong (*dike* and *adikia*) into the cosmic process, and clearly transfers the moral forces of social and political life and its civil struggle into an eternal order. For the use of an abstract concept of time (*chronos*), the parallel to Solon has rightly been drawn, whose reforms will be judged, as he says, "in the court of time" (*en dike chronou*).

Relations between philosophy and society were even more obvious in the aftermath of the Milesians. There was Xenophanes of Colophon, who wrote in verse, and after the age of twenty-five, according to his own words, "tossed his thought about for sixty-seven years, up and down the land of Greece." Thus, he was ninety-two when he wrote this, a poet and philosopher who sang his own songs. He combined the rhapsodic tradition with a social position in which he could outline (11, fr. 1 *VS*) ritual and moral rules for a symposium, that is to say, he was on equal standing with his aristocratic audience. His views in general, however, were radical and revolutionary. He objected to the contemporary overestimation of athletics and the official honors granted to victorious athletes. His main interest was in religion; that is to say, he fought against the popular concepts and beliefs. His attacks on the gods of Homer and Hesiod must have made a strong impact, though they had little influence on the general mind of the Greeks. Here, at last, was the man who could not only think out clearly a world free from mythology, but oppose any form of anthropomorphic gods. "But the mortals think that gods were born and that they had garments and voice and shape like them" (fr. 14 *VS*). He told his audience that black people would worship black gods, that the gods of the Thracians would have blue eyes and red hair (fr. 16 *VS*), even that animals, if they could draw, would draw gods as horses or cattle (fr. 15 *VS*). This anthropological or even zoological approach to religion shows a magnificent freedom of mind, and an interest, growing generally at that time, in ethnological and anthropological knowledge. The rational explanation of myths, though in a very different way, was also pursued by Hecataeus of Miletus. His unphilosophical mind discovered in myth the features of normal human happenings. His chief interest, however, was in geography and ethnography. Herodotus, as we shall see, learnt from him; he can be called the grandfather of history.

Xenophanes' rationalism was rivaled only by his astonishing picture of the one god who is in no way similar to man, either in body or thought (fr. 23 *VS*), who "without toil shakes everything by the thought of his mind" (fr. 25 *VS*)—the last word being *nous,* the central power of Anaxagoras and later philosophers, of which Pindar said (*Nem.* 6.4) that it may make a man similar to the gods. Xenophanes, the wandering philosopher, was the first to preach a kind of spiritual monotheism in Greece; he found successors among both philosophers and poets.

Xenophanes probably died in Italy; also his great contemporary Pythagoras of Samos went and worked there. The link between east and west within the Greek world had grown strong, especially among people of the same social class of aristocrats. Pythagoras left Samos because of Polycrates' despotic rule; he held definitely aristocratic views which led to the foundation at Croton of an exclusive brotherhood. The facts about his life and teaching are obscured partly by the secrecy of the movement, and partly by the large amount of legendary tales. But we can at least say that Pythagoras combined mathematics and mysticism, that his great scientific achievements were accompanied and probably overshadowed by his theory of reincarnation and by the strict rules of abstinence imposed on his followers. What to all appearances was a kind of religious order and a mystery religion, based largely on contemplation and purification, was at the same time a philosophical school, upholding the view of the integral harmony of the world as expressed in numbers.

Pythagoras united in himself two outstanding and almost opposite tendencies of the sixth century, philosophy and natural science on the one hand, intense religious feelings and obscure mysticism on the other. Parmenides, Heraclitus, Empedocles—each in his own distinct way—continued what their predecessors had begun, all of them somehow on both sides of the boundary between cosmological thought and human mystic beliefs. They were the heirs of the archaic age, and the inaugurators of a new age.

It is time now for us briefly to consider the last century of the Archaic Age more generally. The sixth century, even though we leave out for the moment the brilliant part played by Athens (since that belongs to a special lecture), was a rich century, both materially and spiritually. Trade and manufacture were responsible for the production and exchange of goods which raised the standard of living. More people could drink better wine from more beautiful cups, more women could have dresses and cosmetics such as they had not known before, building materials improved, and artists and craftsmen learned to vie with the work imported from abroad; they soon surpassed it. Urban life became more and more important, though private houses were still, and for some time to come, very simple, and the streets narrow and dirty; but intellectual and artistic life was largely concentrated in the cities. This was an additional reason for the slow decline of the aristocracy, of which we have spoken before. Even so the social conventions of the nobles largely determined the culture of the non-nobles, and the countryside still had its say; the economic and not only the economic foundations of most Greek communities remained rural.

It was, for instance, the rural deities, the gods of the earth and the depth beneath it, who—partly under the impact of imported non-Greek cults—were resurrected from ancient traditions that in most cases had never quite ceased to exist. These gods now triumphantly invaded the urban societies where the Olympians had ruled almost unchallenged. Of these new-old gods probably none were more important than Demeter and Dionysus, both ancient deities, both practically banned from epic poetry. They were agrarian gods, gods of fertility, but at the same time bound up with what in general

is called mystery religion. A strong irrational trend of the
Greek mind, always extant, had by then come more into the
open. It was usually a ritual within an existing cult which
provided the individual worshiper with some kind of sublimation, some satisfaction for his personal religious needs.
The cult of Dionysus, whose ecstatic worship in the wild
mountains was, so it seems, already known to Archilochus
(fr. 77 D) and Alcman (fr. 56 P, 37 D), was changed by the
introduction of Thracian mysteries, but gradually acclima-
tized to the more serene Greek climate. Demeter, on her part,
was indissolubly connected with the mysteries of Eleusis,
for which Peisistratus built the first Telesterion, the hall of
worship and mystery rites, which probably stood on the place
of a Mycenaean temple of Demeter. Together with mother
and daughter, Demeter and Kore, but apart from the mysteries, Triptolemus was worshiped as a hero who personified
agriculture as the basis of all civilized life. What was common
to all the mystery cults was that they catered for the individual, regardless of class or status; among the initiates of
Eleusis were not only citizens of all classes, but also slaves.

Ever since Nietzsche, guided by deep intuition as well as
mistaken presuppositions, distinguished between an Apollo-
nian and a Dionysian Greece, more evidence for and more
insight into the darker, un-Homeric, earth-bound, mysterious
side of the Greek mind has become part of modern scholarship. Perhaps nothing is more true of the Greeks, their
politics, their thought, their religion, than the idea of the
"harmony of the opposites," to which Heraclitus gave the
most concise expression: *palintropos harmonie,* a harmony
caused by opposite forces. In one of his most famous, but
also frequently misunderstood fragments (12, fr. 55 *VS*) he
says: "War is the father of everything, the king of all." War
is to him more than the events on a battlefield; it is the
cause of the social differences, of gods and men, free and

slaves, and at the same time the strife of contrasting forces, the metaphysical basis of civilization.

A religious wave swept over Greece during the sixth century. There was the greatly increased prestige of Delphi, the ecstatic worship of Dionysus, the mysticism of the Orphics, the turn which philosophy took in Pythagoreanism, finally the wonder workers and prophets such as Epimenides. As Homer's gods had reflected an aristocratic human society, so the *kosmos* of the philosophers mirrored the political human community. As Homer's gods were the models of anthropomorphic religion, thus the chthonian cults, the mysteries, the Orphic beliefs reflected a divine world beyond human standards. Those who thought of death as simply the end of life, followed by a soulless existence in Hades, found opponents in those to whom the visible body was only the prison of the soul, and the soul's life the true life. The rational and the irrational, the realist and the mystic, the poet and the thinker, the citizen and the artist, but also the nobility and the people, they all testify to the unique wealth of the civilization of the era. From the union of these diverse forces sprang Attic tragedy, and with it the other wonders of the Classical Age.

# III. The Athenian Century

Once again, our story concentrates on Athens. Athens had gained the victories of Marathon and Salamis and had united the Aegean world under her rule; Pericles called her "the school of Hellas"—Athens made the fifth century essentially an Athenian century. I do not forget that Greek civilization flourished at other places as well, and in particular in Southern Italy and Sicily. Nor do I forget the sublime poetry of Pindar. But again and again we find Athens in the center of things, and as I must select, it makes sense to speak now of Athens alone.

Her greatness was based on the work of three men of the sixth century: Solon, Peisistratus, and Cleisthenes. Solon aimed at overcoming the social and economic crisis of Athens by creating a state and society of *eunomia*—that is, of conditions of "good order," of a balanced order under the rule of law, and of good citizenship. It was the same concept that Tyrtaeus had had in Sparta, but the mixture was different. The rigid rule of the Spartiates over the non-Spartiates, Perioeci as well as helots, was carried out by a society of equals (*homoioi*), the *damos* of full citizens; the outcome in practice was oligarchy, and at the same time the end of cultural life. Solon wrote after his reforms (fr. 5 D): "To the demos, I gave such honor as is sufficient for them, neither more nor less; for those who had power and were rich, I took care that they should not suffer undue wrong. There I was, holding a strong shield over both sides and letting neither unjustly prevail over the other." We know that the nobles and wealthy retained their estates and most of their

political power, while the poor peasantry were relieved of
their debts and the threat of enslavement; their revolutionary
demand for the redistribution of land was turned down,
and Solon's law of adoption by testament of a childless man
was only a first small step toward securing the single household against the clan, the first step toward private landed
property. Nevertheless, the lower classes gained decisively.
They had their share in the growing prosperity of Athens,
and they played a part in the people's assembly. Solon knew
about the various ways of making a living (fr. 1.43ff. D); he
had overcome a good many prejudices of the noble class, but
he still believed that man's success finally depended on the
gods (fr. 1.41ff. D). He was not an economist, but a wise
and pious man, later regarded as one of the Seven Wise Men;
slogans attributed to him, stressing the middle path in life
(such as *meden agan*), fit well with everything we know of
him and his work. By aiming at social justice, he set Athens
on the path to democracy, though there was still a considerable way to go. He aimed at securing a balance between
rich and poor, town and country, husbandry and craftsmanship; but this balance remained unstable for some time, because he was largely successful in the political but not in
the social and economic spheres. The noble clans were still
almost undiminished in power and wealth, and the peasants
were soon again in an economic distress. The wonderful
flowering, on the other hand, of black-figured vase painting
owed much to Solon and then to Peisistratus; they supported
the artisans in general and favored the export trade of oil
and thus of pottery. In his successes and his failures Solon
remained the moderate leader who refused to become a
tyrant, that special brand of one-man rule which was very
much the fashion because it alone seemed capable of prevent-
ing the existing society from breaking up completely. Solon
represented that particular spirit, that atmosphere of har-

mony, courage, and moderation which, we think, was typical of the best in classical Athens.

The continued struggle among various groups of noble families and their followers all over Attica, also the dissatisfaction of the peasants who suffered from poverty, defeated Solon's hope that the community would settle down and give his laws and constitution the necessary period of trial. He could not prevent his younger friend Peisistratus from taking advantage of the disunity of the upper class and seizing power, though he barely lived to see him, after two expulsions, firmly and finally established. Peisistratus expelled some of the noble families and distributed their estates among the poor farmers; it was he who, by increased trade, by colonization, and by building work at home, improved the economic position of the lower classes in town. He also organized festivals like the Great Panathenaea and the City Dionysia as a new framework for athletic, musical, and dramatic performances and competitions, obviously intended to bind all sections of Athenian citizens more closely together, and in particular to make the rural folk visit the city. He also inspired a definite text of Homer for the popular recitals of the rhapsodes. It was a full-scale program, based on the idea of raising the cultural level and increasing the status of the non-noble population. The fact that one man was in power was in itself a cause for an intensified leveling among the various strata of society.

It is difficult to overestimate what Peisistratus did for Athens. When in 510 B.C., through the misrule of his son Hippias and the intervention by Sparta, tyranny was brought to an end, the stage was set for the Alcmaeonid Cleisthenes, the leader of the antityrannical and antioligarchic opposition, to build a state and a society fit for democracy. He destroyed the power of the noble clans, though he made no attempt at destroying the aristocracy itself or its religious and cultural

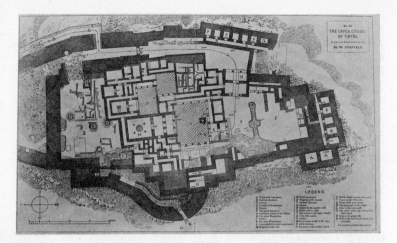

FIGURE 1. Tiryns. Map of the upper citadel. Mostly late Helladic III (c. 1400-1200 B.C.). Shows the enormous strength of the fortifications and the two megara of the palace (M, O).

FIGURE 2. Mycenae. Interior of beehive tomb ("Treasury of Atreus"). Late Helladic III.

FIGURE 3. Cnossus. Fresco: bull game with male and female athletes. Late Minoan I (c. 1550-1450 B.C.).

FIGURE 4. Cnossus. Fresco: ladies as spectators. Late Minoan I.

FIGURE 5. Hagia Triada. Sarcophagus. Procession with lyre-player. Late Minoan III (c. 1400 B.C.).

FIGURE 6. Cnossus. Fayence. Minoan goddess (or priestess?) with snakes. Middle Minoan III (c. 1600 B.C.).

FIGURE 7. Dipylon Oenochoe. Frieze with Aktorione-Moleone (*Il.* 11.709), fighting twins in one body. Second half of eighth century B.C.

FIGURE 8. Dipylon Krater. Funeral: chariots with warriors in procession. Second half of eighth century B.C.

FIGURE 9. Dipylon Krater. Funeral: fight over beached ship. Second half of eighth century B.C.

FIGURE 10. Dipylon Oenochoe. Shipwreck (of Odysseus?). Second half of eighth century B.C.

FIGURE 11. Frieze from Dipylon Vase, showing warriors with different kinds of shields; in the middle is the curious one mentioned in the text. Cf. The shields in fig. 8.

FIGURE 12. François Vase (Krater of Cleitias and Ergotimos). About 570 B.C.

FIGURE 13. Attic    rf.    Neck-Amphora.
Rhapsode. By the Kleophrades painter, c. 490-
480 B.C.

FIGURE 14.    Attic rf. Cup.
Man and boy as lovers.
By Makron, c. 490-480 B.C.

FIGURE 15. Laconian Cup. King Arkesilas of Cyrene supervising loading of ship. Sixth century B.C.

FIGURE 16. Laconian Cup. Warriors carrying the dead. Sixth century B.C.

FIGURE 17. Attic bf. Lekythos. Hoplomachia with onlookers (umpires?). Late sixth century B.C.

FIGURE 18. Attic rf. Cup. Boys at lessons. By Duris, c. 480 B.C.

FIGURE 19. Marble Head. Kore. Late sixth century B.C.

FIGURE 20. Marble statue. Kore, dedicated by Euthydikos. Late sixth century B.C.

FIGURE 21. Marble statue. Kore.
Late sixth century B.C.

FIGURE 22. Attic marble statue.
Kouros, c. 600 B.C.

FIGURE 23. Attic rf. Amphora. Aristocratic youths with Apollo statue. By Andokides painter, 530-520 B.C.

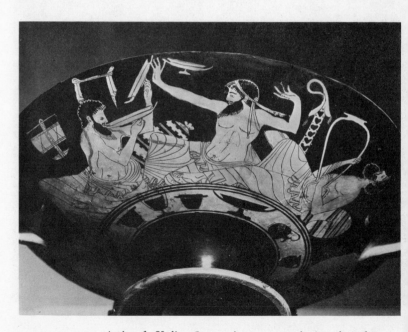

FIGURE 24. Attic rf. Kylix. Symposium, man playing kottabos, c. 490 B.C.

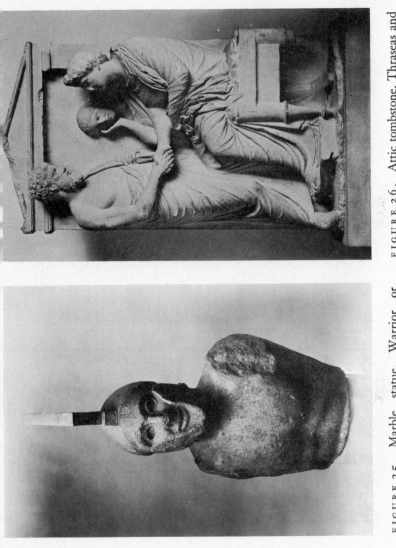

FIGURE 25. Marble statue. Warrior or armed runner ("Leonidas"), c. 490-480 B.C.

FIGURE 26. Attic tombstone. Thraseas and Euandria. Middle fourth century B.C.

FIGURE 27. Attic rf. Amphora. Comic chorus of knights. Middle sixth century B.C.

FIGURE 28. Etruscan Bronze, fibula Praenestina. Second half of seventh century B.C.

FIGURE 29. Etruscan Bronze. She-wolf. Sixth/fifth century B.C.

FIGURE 30. Etruscan Terracotta Sarcophagus. Married couple. Second half of sixth century B.C.

FIGURE 31. Etruscan head, from sarcophagus. Third century B.C.

FIGURE 32. Roman portrait. Marble. First century B.C.

traditions. He called his state *isonomia,* equality in law, the opposite of *eunomia.* His "new order" became the lasting basis of the further development of Athenian democracy. But this democracy almost forgot him. The heroes who were believed to have liberated Athens and given her *isonomia* were, according to the popular drinking song and to the statues erected to their memory and their cult, two young aristocrats, Harmodius and Aristogeiton, a pair of lovers, who in 514 B.C. were killed after murdering the harmless Hipparchus; they only succeeded in strengthening the tyranny of his brother Hippias. It took four years before Hippias was expelled, and more before democracy was truly started by Cleisthenes. The cult of the tyrannicides together with the neglected and partially distorted memory of Cleisthenes is a curious symbol of democratic Athens. Gratitude is a rare virtue in political life, though I am inclined to regard what happened to the memory of Cleisthenes as the work of the noble clans who were hostile to the Alcmaeonids and eager to retain a hold on official democracy.

Alcmaeon, a physician at Croton, though probably not a Pythagorean, also speaks of *isonomia.* He contrasts (14, fr. 4 *VS*) *isonomia* and monarchy in the human body; the one as "the uniform mixture of qualities" means health, the other, when one quality is prominent, means illness. The contrast is clearly taken over from politics, and it is likely that Alcmaeon, roughly a contemporary of Cleisthenes, had heard of his use of the word *isonomia,* expressing the opposition to monarchical *tyrannis.* Analogies between microcosm and macrocosm were fairly often drawn at that time, though ever since Anaximander it was usual to compare the universe, not the individual, with the community of men. It is significant that now natural science, the science of man, entered the arena. Alcmaeon is only one example among many that shows how the structure and the spirit of the *polis,* and especially of democracy, invaded other fields of intellectual and artistic activities.

In our times we would think that all this was largely a matter of education; but education in the modern sense was a late growth in Greece. Simonides said (fr. 53 D): "Polis teaches Man"; he did not think of state schools and the like, he thinks of man as *zoon politikon,* as a member of the political community. Education in the sense of deliberate instruction started from the military needs of a warlike society. Thucydides (1.6) tells us that Athens was the first state to do away with a life under arms. Military training changed into athletic training; *hoplomachia,* a competition in fully armed fighting, remained as a survival (see fig. 17), and was even in the late fifth century, as is shown by the beginning of Plato's *Laches,* still regarded as a main part of education. Otherwise there were the usual "sports" in palaestra and gymnasium, and in addition *mousike,* which meant poetry, song, and dance. It still was the education of an upper class, originally given by fathers and elders, later by professional teachers, mostly slaves. It was the education of a gentleman, or in Greek terms: of a *kaloskagathos,* a combination, as I believe, of a boy's beauty and a man's bravery and dignity. With the rise of a wealthy middle class, athletic and musical education, the background of Athenian civilization, became a matter for many more people. In the late fifth century, the notorious "Old Oligarch," a reactionary partisan pamphleteer, could write (Ps.-Xen., *Ath. pol.* 2.10): "Some of the rich have gymnasia and bathrooms and dressing rooms of their own; but the people have built for their own private use many palaestras, dressing rooms and bathrooms, and the mob enjoys this more than the few wealthy do." This may be irony, but it is nevertheless the truth. The aristocrats certainly resented (as Theognis, Pindar, or Aristophanes, in the

*Clouds,* shows) the social and cultural ambitions of the *nouveaux riches,* even more those of the masses.

The picture as drawn so far is not complete. There was, on the one hand, in the education of the noble youth a very definite tendency to form a boy's character, to teach him a certain code of ethical behavior, to make him a true *aner agathos,* a man worthy of his ancestors and fit to serve the community. On the other hand, the introduction of ostracism around 500 B.C. shows that most Athenians could write and usually even spell. There must have been schools, not only individual teachers, to teach music and poetry, and above all the three R's, and indeed there is evidence for this, though scanty (see fig. 18). Herodotus tells us (6.27) that the collapse of a roof in Chios killed one hundred and twenty schoolboys, certainly a large number; that was shortly before the battle of Lade in 496 B.C. Even Spartan boys learned to read. The Athenians were, in general, better educated than other Greeks, and had, as we shall see, higher intellectual interests.

Poetry at Athens had a lull during the sixth century, while painting and sculpture went vigorously ahead. This reminds us of the fact that the various branches of intellectual and artistic life did not always flourish simultaneously. There did not have to be any external reasons for this. Foreign poets like Anacreon and Simonides came to the court of the Peisistratids, but no native poet of importance emerged until Thespis, who started tragedy, of which I shall have more to say in a moment. When we think of Athens before and after 500 B.C., we should mention those rather charming stanzas sung, just like songs by Alcaeus or Anacreon, at the *symposia* (see fig. 24). These were the *skolia,* with their praise of noble virtues, their enjoyment of life, but also the praise of the tyrannicides and the appeal to various gods.

Though they are not great poetry, they provide quite a good picture of the mind and life of the upper class.

The same period is even more impressively represented by the works of the painters and sculptors. Vase painting, after gradually changing over to the red-figured style, reached its highest perfection. Apart from mythological scenes, it is the life of the upper-class youth that is mainly represented, though we also have pictures of peasants and craftsmen at work. As to sculpture, I should like to remind you of the wonderful Acropolis Museum, where most of the sculptures belong to the time before 480, when the Acropolis was burnt by the Persians. Among the statues there are the many votive figures of young women, known as *korai* (see figs. 19–21). Many of them show very individual features, though it is doubtful whether we may call them portraits. Certain is that these highly sophisticated young ladies, with their elaborate dresses, are examples of an elegant and graceful upper class. We should like to think that fathers dedicated statues of their daughters to Athena. Ionian influence, even Ionian artists, played a part, which resulted in the refinement and elaborate appearance of some of the statues, though gradually the Athenian sense of simplicity and harmony took over. Earlier sculptors had discovered the beauty of the male nude. The statues of young men, often called Apollines or *Kouroi* (see fig. 22), dating from the early sixth century onward, cannot deny their descent from Egyptian and Cretan predecessors, but as they grew more realistic and came to life, they reflected the essential part played by the palaestra and athletics in the lives of the noble youths. About the same time, it had become the custom at Olympia to run the stadium race without a loin cloth. Slowly, as we have seen, the shape of the female body was discovered, if mainly through the folds of the garments. Only exceptionally, in vase paintings and—significantly—with some small bronzes of Spartan girls, do we find women depicted in the nude. In the different attitude of the artists toward the sexes, different social conditions are reflected. I abstain from explaining the archaic smile as a sign of social amiability.

The attitude toward the sexes reached an unexpected climax and reversion when the young aristocrats, the dandies of the day, adopted feminine fashions for themselves, wearing their hair long or in a "bun," displaying golden trinkets and fine linen chitons, and holding flowers in their hands (see fig. 23). This predominance of the feminine element would not have been possible without the existence at Athens of a *jeunesse dorée,* as we can easily imagine it in the years before the Persian wars. Besides, it reveals an artistic mannerism which was an Ionian import and could be regarded as the leave-taking of the Archaic Age. Archaeologists distinguish a number of styles, but artistic styles are not a safe guide for chronology and history, although in one way or another they do express tendencies of the time. One thing is certain: after the richness and the mannerism of the late sixth century, a new simplicity prevailed, and men's minds turned to more essential things. The Ionian revolt with the burning of Miletus made a deep impression; aristocrats and common people alike went to war against the Persian invaders. The hoplites won at Marathon, but their leader was Miltiades, who belonged to one of the oldest clans; victory was due to the upper and middle classes of democracy. Ten years later, Miltiades' son Cimon dedicated his bridle to Athena, as a sign that the noble cavalry had ceased to play a part in war. Salamis was won by both the oarsmen and the hoplites on board ship; the former came from the lower classes whom Solon had admitted to the assembly. They now shared in the defense of the country, and complete democracy—complete as far as citizens were concerned—became inevitable. Cimon, the popular aristocrat, was followed by the aristocratic democrat Pericles in the leadership of Athens and of an empire which they both were building up. For the first time in the history of mankind, the ideas of liberty and equality gained full political status, though it was not *liberté, égalité, fraternité*. The brotherhood of mankind was not even in the offing, but it meant a great deal that the principles of freedom and equality before the law materialized, if only for the citizens of Athens. It was an ideal, expressed by Thucydides in Pericles' famous Funeral Speech, an ideal which had its far-reaching effects, however imperfect the reality was and still is.

We ask what corresponded to the political greatness in the fields of intellect and art? The pediments of the Aphaea temple at Aegina with their fighting hoplites or the so-called "Leonidas" (see fig. 25) are worthy contemporaries of the men who fought the Persians. Then peace came, Panhellenic peace, and nothing in contemporary art can equal the majestic beauty of the pediments of the Zeus temple at Panhellenic Olympia. Athens still produced remarkable art, foreshadowing the age of Pheidias and the Parthenon, but it was the theater that made this period of Athenian civilization unique. The origins of Attic tragedy and comedy have been widely discussed from the most different points of view. I shall not add to that discussion, but will mention one fact that is important in our context. Several kinds of rustic ritual dances and choral songs were, so it seems, the ancestors of tragic and comic choruses, and they were favored and fostered by tyrants such as Peisistratus or Cleisthenes of Sicyon, as a means of opposing the aristocracy and pleasing the common people. Attic vases show some choruses, many comic or satyrs, but all parts of the Dionysiac cult (see fig. 27). In its various forms, this cult belonged to the lower classes, mainly, though not exclusively, to the peasantry. Taking tragedy and comedy together, we can say that one of the spiritually and intellectually highest forms of literary art developed as the sublimation of popular worship with its music and ecstasy, its absurdities and obscenities. Though the Dithyrambus, the song to Dionysus, seems to have been the chief ancestor of the tragic chorus, the contents of the plays are as a rule non-Dionysiac. It cannot be ascertained to what extent the performances at the Great Dionysia were still regarded as an act of worship, and how the plays fitted into the framework of a Dionysiac festival, but the priest of Dionysus had his seat in the first row in the theater. The contents of the plays are myths, either of Homeric heritage (and Homer's name stood for more than only the *Iliad* and *Odyssey*) or connected with the cult of local gods and heroes. The special myth had to be explained and, more than that, it had to come to life; this was how spoken lines and dialogue came into being. It meant something beyond merely literary developments. The slogan "democracy is discussion" is modern, but it is essentially true for all times. With the invention of the dramatic dialogue, the poet was able to introduce religious and ethical, even political problems (not only themes), and to discuss them on the stage. The people on the tiers of the theater had their emotional and intellectual share in these problems, the poet more than ever belonged to the community, and in a new and, as it were, democratic form, without any didactic purpose, he once again was the teacher of his people.

I know that the "educational" aspect of Attic drama is not a fashionable point of view today; perhaps I may say a few general words about our attitude toward Greek poetry and, in particular, tragedy. The argument is that modern literary critics generally deal with, say, Shakespeare or Schiller purely as dramatists and poets, and do not much bother about Elizabethan or late eighteenth-century society. Though this is no longer quite true, it seems legitimate to ask whether we cannot do the same with the Greeks. Many say we can.

Earlier scholars often did indeed the opposite by neglecting
the poetical and dramatic issues facing the poet; since then
we have learned a good deal about his technique and his art.
I am not so sure how much we have gained in real understanding, however subtle—and in fact subjective—modern
analysis frequently is. The Athenian tragedian wrote for the
theater, that is to say, for an audience practically identical
with all the citizens, and they regarded a poet as a member
of their community as well as a mouthpiece of divine wisdom. I doubt whether those ordinary citizens who had to
judge the plays at Athens knew much of the tragedian's
dramatic technique; what they did know was the general
impact, moral and emotional, on the audience. No doubt,
they sometimes reached surprising decisions, but who are we,
with our so much weaker knowledge of the poet's aims and
effects, with hardly any knowledge of dance and music, both
so essential—who are we to do better than the Athenians
themselves?

Myth was early history to the Greeks, besides being an
expression of religious belief. It was also something almost
contemporary; its story and its religious meaning could
change according to the whims of a poet and the trends of
contemporary thought, it could even be influenced by political
events, alliances, or enmities of the moment. Allusions to
the problems of the day could enter the mythical story,
though we must be careful not to read too much actuality
into a play. How closely myth and present time were connected is clearly shown when the sole subject of a tragedy
was about the immediate past. Phrynichus wrote his play
"The Capture of Miletus," which moved the audience to
outbursts of passionate sorrow (Hdt. 6.27), and in the
seventies he and Aeschylus wrote plays about the great
Persian War. This was only a few years after the event. We
still read the *Persae* of Aeschylus; here the natural pride and

prejudices of a victorious people are raised to a higher level, in fact, to a myth, in which the *hybris* and the humanity of the enemy are seen with magnanimous understanding. The chorus as the true tragic hero of the play suffers for its loyalty to an impious and wicked king, implying how well deserved was the victory of a people fighting for its freedom and its gods.

The development of comedy ran on similar lines. Primitive Attic and Dorian elements joined in creating a loose dramatic form in which conventional comic features and mythical parody combined with political and personal satire. Obscene jokes and the ridiculing of the bystanders had been a feature of early phallic processions; they and other Dionysiac features could appear, but on the whole, fifth-century comedy, in particular its standing item of the battle of words, the *agon,* were the farcical counterpart to the serious discussions in the assembly and in tragedy. In comedy, the principle of freedom of speech (*parrhesia*) was carried to consequences which aroused opposition among the very standard bearers of democracy, but in general it was a good thing that poet and people had a wonderful opportunity to let off steam. Thus, comedy makes fun of reality, while starting on a fanciful flight into the never-never world. The background world of real life, however, is always there; no play—whether tragedy or comedy—was performed at Athens that did not reflect the ways and the spirit of the Athenian people.

A well-known story connects the three great tragedians with the battle of Salamis. Aeschylus fought in it as he had done at Marathon, Sophocles as a youth danced in the victory dance, and Euripides is supposed to have been born that very day. In a sense the story is true: Aeschylus' mind was formed by the years of the Persian wars; in danger and victory he recognized Zeus' rule of justice. The adult life of Sophocles began in the postwar years; he was the representative of the harmony and tragedy of classical Athens. Euripides lived, as it were, in a different Athens, a city of disruption and defeat, even though he and Sophocles died in the same year. The life and work of the three tragedians reflect the whole perturbed history of fifth-century Athens, and the changing thoughts and moods of the people. Attic tragedy, like Goethe's *Faust,* took the measure of men and gods as a whole—"from Heaven through the World to Hell." It would be far beyond my purpose here, and the limits of my ability as well, to follow the three poets on their different and yet cognate journeys, all three of them always in search of a deeper understanding of man and his responsibility toward his fellow men and toward the gods. One predominant trend, however, that I ought to mention is the ever-growing insight into the character of men (and women) who are tragic because they are, like Ajax or Oedipus, guilty in a deeper sense, lonely and in need of human understanding. At the end of the century the emotional relations between man and man or man and woman had become the real subject matter. With Euripides, at a time when the individual more and more appeared as the center of thought, psychology was born.

We ask what was the reaction of the audience. I have already pointed out that the Athenian theater was really a people's theater. It was a fixed rule that the audience, after having been excited and moved by three tragedies, could relax at the immediately following satyr drama. If they enjoyed some plays more than others and had, for instance, to get used to the "modern" trend in Euripides (who was never so popular as after his death), if they generally enjoyed tragedy just as much as the burlesque of the satyr play and the wit and obscenity of comedy, it did mean that they, a large and representative cross-section of the Athenian people, were a very special audience. There can be no doubt about the interest the Athenians took in the new variations of the mythical stories, and in literature and literary criticism generally. Comedy is full of literary allusions, quotations and parodies; and Aristophanes' *Frogs,* performed in the last years of the Peloponnesian War, at a time of anguish and distress, is concerned with the literary and religious qualities of the tragedians, albeit with the object of finding in the greatest tragedian—and that is most significant—at the same time the savior of the state. The *Frogs* confirms both the literary interest of the audience and the close bond between theater and community. Greek tragedies and comedies belonged to one common world, and they had more in common than the fact that they provided good theater.

Tragedy and comedy were true Athenian growths, whatever their Dorian or other predecessors. The astonishing union between Attic dialogue and the songs of the chorus in Doric dialect was a purely Athenian invention. Most of the tragedians and practically all poets of Old Comedy were Athenian citizens, though slowly the greatness of the Attic theater attracted foreign poets as well. Probably the first was Ion of Chios, contemporary and friend of Sophocles. The appearance of foreign dramatists was part of a more general story of which we shall speak later. One fact about the origin of the tragedians remains remarkable. The three great men created a kind of succession by sons and relatives. This was not simply due to heredity (which at any rate would be surprising), for not all of these successors were direct descendants. Such a family tradition might sometimes exist among politicians, it was institutionally connected with certain priesthoods, but above all it was typical for craftsmanship. I have no doubt that the writing of tragedies or comedies could to some extent be learned. It is unlikely that any one of the descendants, whose plays have not survived, was a genius, but they must have learned their craft well enough. Aeschylus' son won victories over Sophocles and Euripides, and his

nephew even defeated the *Oedipus Rex*. The taste and bias of
the judges will have played their part in these verdicts, but
they usually seem to have expressed the *vox populi*. There
was a professionalism, displayed in the complicated technique
of the plays and in their production; the poet usually was
the *chorodidaskalos,* the teacher and trainer of chorus and
actors, of dancing and acting—we should say, the producer.
It is significant that the poet frequently needed, or at least
was given, protection and help by a patron, probably also
the money for the production. Such a relation could become
part of politics, as in the case of Themistocles' patronage of
Phrynichus; but we also know of Cratinus' praise for Cimon's
hospitality, and of Pericles' friendly relations with men like
Sophocles and Anaxagoras. A friendship between statesman
and poet (or thinker) went beyond traditional patronage,
and it is possible that it was considered unconventional. Even
so, a poet's professionalism was for Greek opinion something
different from that of a sculptor or painter; when Pericles
made Pheidias his friend, the aristocrat the manual craftsman, he did something very unusual.

Eternal witnesses of the Periclean age are the buildings on
the Acropolis. They were part of an extensive building program which followed the policy of Peisistratus, not only at
Athens but also in Eleusis and other Attic shrines such as
Brauron. We are expressly told that Pericles built to alleviate
the unemployment caused during the forties by the return
of the soldiers from the first war with Sparta (Plut., *Per.* 12).
This is confirmed by the fact that about the same time many
cleruchies and colonies were sent out; of one at least, Brea
in Thrace, we know that it was confined to the lower classes
(Tod, no. 44.41). Building activities continued with short
interruptions throughout the Peloponnesian War, and the
Erechtheum was erected even in its last phase. Records still
in existence show that at that time citizens, metics—resident

foreigners—and slaves were employed in the work on equal standing. The losses in the war, and the fact that many men were on active service, will have been the reason for using noncitizens. Even so, unemployment relief was only one of Pericles' motives for the building program. Athens was the capital of an empire; she was responsible for the freedom of the seas and for keeping the Persians out of the Aegean. After the Peace of Callias (449 B.C.) Pericles collected from the tributes of the allies a reserve fund which now served a peaceful purpose. But there were other resources as well, and in the later phase of the war the tributes had been reduced to a mere trickle. It is a mistaken view that the great buildings were simply built with the blood and sweat of the allies. They naturally resented the paying of tribute, but less so than the interference in their internal affairs, and many remained loyal, even when Athens was losing the war. Each year they sent ambassadors to the Great Dionysia, and we can be sure that they admired the works of Ictinus and Pheidias just as much as those of Sophocles. Their admiration may have been mixed with envy, but it would be wrong to assume they had not shown pride in their leading city. It was Pericles' intention to make Athens beautiful, worthy of her political greatness, and the Athenians were certainly proud of their city. This popular feeling is strikingly expressed by one of the comic poets, Lysippus (fr. 7 K, p. 702), who wrote when the Parthenon and Propylaea were already standing on the Acropolis; he says: "If you haven't seen Athens, you're a blockhead; if you have seen it and are not struck, you're an ass; if you are pleased to go away, you're a pack horse"—a man without higher interests, a philistine.

To some extent, a man's life was bound to his family, though family life, as we understand it, hardly existed. Girls were not educated; they only learned the arts of housekeeping. Marriage was a matter of paternal wishes and economic considerations. Women only slowly gained a more independent position, and by and by examples of marital love became more frequent, until in New Comedy love matches were the rule. In the fifth century, we see little of that except when life ended. In the pictures of the dead on white *lekythoi* and tombstones we find examples of love and tenderness (see fig. 26). There we also find a reflection of the personal attachment between the mistress and the slave girls. And soon after, the full beauty of the nude female body was discovered; with Praxiteles' Cnidian Aphrodite a new artistic ideal was created, though socially it is significant that it was the hetaera Phryne who served as his model. At the same time the elegant ladies of the Tanagra terracottas give some indication of the social role of wives and daughters in the bourgeoisie of the fourth century.

I have mentioned slaves sharing in the building work; I have hardly spoken of them otherwise. Is that justifiable in what the Marxists today call a "slave-holders' society"? Slavery, of course, was a fact, but few periods of history, if any, down to our own times were free of slavery, even though it might not always be called by that name. The degree of personal freedom and prosperity many slaves enjoyed, especially at Athens, was remarkably high; a minority had a good chance of eventually gaining freedom. Athenian economy or politics was never dominated by the slave problem, though it remains true that without slaves, in particular the badly treated slaves in the mines, the citizens of Athens would never have been able to dedicate so much time to their state or to cultural activities. The metics also contributed to the prosperity of Athens and the independence of her citizens, though most of the latter had to work in order to live. Athens was a great center, and more important than slaves and metics was her indomitable spirit. It was in the years of Pericles' ascendancy that Sophocles produced the *Antigone*

with the famous chorus: "Many things are formidable, but
nothing is more formidable than man." The poet admires
man's great achievements, but warns men not to abandon the
laws of justice. The independence of the individual was a
serious danger to moral standards, and the pious poet turns
against the modern spirit. It is not by chance that his song
alludes to the famous myth of the origin of human civilization as told by Protagoras, the first and foremost of the
Sophists.

Athens attracted more foreigners of cultural standing than
any other city. There were sculptors from Ionia or the
Peloponnese, there were poets and writers. Some stayed for
a short time, as, for instance, Simonides and Pindar, others
for many years or for good. Herodotus, after all his traveling,
went to Athens and was on friendly terms with Sophocles;
his relation to Pericles is ambiguous, but he went out to
Thurii, Pericles' Panhellenic colony—Panhellenic, that is to
say, under Athenian leadership. Herodotus became a citizen
of Thurii; whether he later returned to Athens and died
there is uncertain. He wrote in a slightly mixed dialect,
essentially Ionian, and he mentions Hecataeus of Miletus as
a predecessor whom he wants to correct and surpass. In the
motley arrangement and the richness of his material he still
belongs to Ionia and the archaic age; this is only natural
when we think of the late development of prose writing,
compared with poetry and art. He is deeply religious, but
combines contradictory views: absolute rule of divine provi-
dence and envy of the gods as well as divine justice and
human *hybris,* simple piety as well as rationalistic explanation. Again we trace the archaic legacy, but also an unmistakable influence of "modern" times. The mixture is almost
certainly a result of the course of Herodotus' life, which was
a continuous journey not only through the Mediterranean
world, but also through societies belonging to different

epochs. He claimed to display the results of *historie*—we might call it research—curiosity for the conditions and actions of men everywhere. *Historie,* the search for truth, was born in Ionia, but Herodotus, beside all his ethnography, geography, and story-telling, thanks to his genius and the greatest experience of his life, was able to give the word the meaning it preserved for all future; he recognized the historical theme of the conflict between East and West which culminated in the Persian Wars. This was not only a great subject, it was for Herodotus also a divinely ordered plan, the framework to which all individual actions and characters were subordinated. Herodotus stressed the great part played by Athens, but he knew of the share of Sparta and others as well. While his interests were Panhellenic, his trend impartial, his deeper feelings pious and nonpolitical, he knew about Cleisthenes' work and praised *isonomia* as the "most beautiful of names." He indeed realized many of the interconnections between personal, social, and political motives and events. Not a blind admirer of Athens or of Pericles, he probably owed his historical insight largely to the spirit of Periclean Athens. He was accepted into the circle of the intellectual elite at Athens. The "School of Hellas" taught also *patrem historiae.*

It seems right to mention in this context the non-Athenian Hippocratic book *About Winds, Waters, Places,* in which a description of the impact on man by the natural environment is followed by the contrasting pictures of the nature of Asia and Europe. In both parts we feel the author's affinity to Herodotus, but there are definite differences. Hippocrates, if he is the author, had imbibed the scientific spirit of the age; he also shows a feeling for the Greek landscape. We know that it shaped the Greeks, gods and men. No Greek temple was built without an eye for its setting in the landscape. Many pictures of girls show them with flowers in their hands. From Homer's similes to Euripides' chorus praising

the air and the sky of Attica (*Medea* 824ff.), and down to
the plane trees on the bank of Ilissus in Plato's *Phaedrus,*
there are rare but eloquent witnesses to the innate Greek
love for the beauty of their country. Their feelings were not,
like ours, expressed through romantic ideas; Socrates even
found that places and trees could not teach him anything
(*Phdr.* 230D). But all is "full of the gods," and the social
picture would be incomplete without mentioning the mountains and forests, the rivers and streams, the trees and flowers,
the air, the sky, and the sea of Greece.

Apart from Herodotus, the most important foreigners in
fifth-century Athens were the Sophists. Protagoras of Abdera
arrived toward the middle of the century; for a time he went
to Thurii as a lawgiver; there, if not earlier, Herodotus must
have met him. Even he, a man of religious convictions, learnt
something from the new teaching of the Sophists; for others
it meant a complete change of outlook. Once more, Greek
intellectual life was startled and enriched by professionals.
The Sophists came from all corners of the Greek world to
Athens, wandering from city to city and taking high fees
for their teaching; their pupils were almost exclusively the
young men of the upper classes. Among the Sophists there
were considerable differences in method and thought, but
there was a common denominator, and that is what really
counts. They taught a new kind of popular philosophy, a
philosophy with man, and indeed political man, in its center.
Protagoras in his *homo-mensura* sentence (fr. 1 *VS:* "Man is
the measure of all things, of those existing how they are, of
those non-existing how they are not") stated that all percep-
tion was subjective. Combined with his skepticism about the
gods (fr. 4 *VS:* "I do not know that they exist or that they do
not exist"), this teaching ended in ethical relativism, if not
with him, certainly with his disciples. At the same time, men
like Gorgias and Prodicus preached a Panhellenism which at

first probably weakened Polis patriotism rather than actually strengthened the feeling of Greek solidarity. The whole development culminated in the opposition of *nomos* and *physis,* *nomos* being custom, man-made convention, traditional law, while *physis* was what nature has fixed, independently of human interference, either the character and will of the individual or general concepts of humanity, free from political frontiers and even from the difference between Greeks and barbarians. Each people has its own *nomos,* as Herodotus (3.38) shows by comparing the customs of doing away with the dead; we remember that in the same question of burial Antigone followed the "unwritten laws" of the gods. Heraclitus (12, fr. 114 *VS*) spoke of the divine *nomos* from which all human *nomoi* were nourished. Behind his world of continuous change and strife was the moral unity granted by what we might call the law of nature. It is possible that the whole trend of thought started from Parmenides' contrast between belief (*doxa*) and truth (*aletheia*), but it left the sphere of pure philosophy and with the Sophists plunged into the waters of educational and political questions. A twofold development can be discerned by which human tradition and Polis law were contrasted either by the concept of a higher law (religious or natural) or by the nature of the individual. The latter directly led to the view that right is what is to the advantage of the stronger, in short that might is right. The individual put forward his theoretical claim to power, regardless of society.

You will easily understand that these were not merely theoretical issues. The Sophists were, above all, teachers. We know little of their writings, while their general activities are chiefly recorded by Plato, who was hostile and who gave them their dubious reputation. Even so, enough is known to give us their right measure, and I cannot describe them better than by saying that they were the first professors, ancestors we today need not be ashamed of. It is not their philosophy that counted, but their teaching. They have been called the first humanists; they could be called the first educationalists, who regarded nature, instruction, and practice as the three basic elements of education. Nature (*physis*) was the great new discovery, instruction might include the most various subjects, practice was chiefly rhetorical exercise. It was a largely formal education centered on the needs of state and society. The Sophists taught the "art of politics" (*politike techne*) to the wealthy intelligentsia, who all, or almost all, wished to go into politics. They claimed to be able to teach them how to speak, how to discuss and persuade, and to know the facts of political life. In a democratic society men were needed who fulfilled their personal aims as well as their duty to the community, by being capable of leading or at least influencing the popular assembly or the popular courts. The old aristocratic education, though still in existence, was out of touch with the realities of contemporary life, but it was largely the same leading class which governed the democratic state. Aristocratic *arete* (a word we translate badly as "virtue") as the aim of education was replaced by the ideal of political *arete*. There were charlatans among the Sophists, and much of their teaching was a kind of show business; but they not only met a real need, they also created a revolution in the Greek mind. Without making exaggerated claims, as is sometimes done, we can say that their new ways of thought, their independence from religious and political traditions, their theory and practice of oratory, and their refined methods in the use of language, inaugurated a new epoch. They were helped by the development of science, in particular medicine and mathematics, and by rationalistic and materialistic trends in philosophy; but they would never have succeeded to the extent they did without their own almost naïve optimism. They were the leading spirits of their time. It is proof of their astonishing impact that men such as Pericles, Thucydides, and Euripides were very much under their influence.

One particular point may perhaps be mentioned. There was a growing interest in searching for the true purpose of a man's life. What to Solon had been simply different professions could, as it were, become the fundamental difference between an intellectual and a practical way of life. These are the ancestors of the *vita contemplativa* and the *vita activa,* though in fifth-century society it meant the first emergence only of a stratum of society chiefly concerned with intellectual matters, an educated class. The Sophists had a great deal to do with the formation of that class.

A special word must be said about Thucydides, aristocrat by descent and conviction, but at the same time a rational and philosophical mind who had deeply thought about the events through which he lived. He discarded all supranatural influences and discovered the secrets of historical criticism and also the ways of power politics. His Sophistic training and his knowledge of rational, especially medical, science were of the greatest importance in shaping his mind, but his genius rose above all scholastic training. The admirer of Pericles and the enemy of radical democracy wrote most of his work in exile. There he learned to look at things free from narrow patriotism and free from traditional bonds. As the contemporary of Euripides he also gained psychological insight and a feeling of life's tragedy. He became the first historian to combine art and science, and the man who wrote with equal clarity on the greatness and the failure of Athens.

One of our main sources for the Sophistic movement is Aristophanes' *Clouds.* There we have the *agon* between the Just and the Unjust Logos, which also reflected a contrast between old and young, and between upper and middle class. Although the new education demanded elaborate training and great expense, it was not an esoteric movement. The doctrines spread, theoretical books were published, and even the "man in the street" was not unacquainted with them. Though mainly a privilege of the wealthy, others learned as well. The Athenians were far too interested in all matters of language and literature not to be impressed by politicians who used the new methods. In a splendid simplification, politicians were henceforth generally known as "orators." On the other hand, with the spread of the new education, there began to grow up, as already indicated, a new class which was no longer distinguished by descent or wealth, but by education. This was a lengthy process, reaching far into the future, but it meant something to have inaugurated that educated class which was to lead Greek society through the Hellenistic Age and toward a decisive influence on Rome and her empire. The spirit of this class is reflected in the development of literature and art; the growing realism of both foreshadowed a society in which ultimately the individual was of greater importance than the community.

Aristophanes, behind all his clowning and his high- or low-brow fun, was voicing the feelings of the conservative upper class no less than the ordinary people; he makes it clear that there was at least as much criticism of as enthusiasm for the new teaching, in particular because it meant an attack on the old religion. Those who learned most from the Sophists were the flower of Athenian youth. You will remember that the two charges brought against Socrates were the introduction of new gods and the corruption of the young. It was Socrates whom Aristophanes, twenty-four years before his trial, selected as his target in the *Clouds,* his satire on the Sophists. Our views on Socrates are normally centered on the tragedy of his death, but by then he had been teaching in his own manner for forty years or more. How was it possible that the comedian, and probably public opinion in general, took Socrates as a Sophist, indeed as the arch-Sophist—the same man whom Plato depicts as the most formidable opponent of the Sophists?

Like the Sophists themselves, Socrates was of middle-class origin; his father was a mason, his mother a midwife. They must have left their son some money, since he served as a hoplite, and later did nothing to earn a living. In contrast to the Sophists, he never accepted money for his teaching, a teaching which showed nothing of what we may call professorial status. Accosting people in the street and asking awkward questions, he was well known to most Athenians, probably as a public nuisance. He shared with the Sophists the dialectic method; his pupils were largely of the same class of aristocratic youth as those taught by the Sophists; he too thought that virtue could be taught, as in his view it was knowledge; he too—at least as most people understood him—turned against traditional religion. There was some justification for popular resentment, especially as among his pupils were men like Alcibiades and Critias, the worst enemies of democracy.

The real importance of Socrates is, of course, something quite different. He knew that he knew not. This is the first decisive and difficult step toward true knowledge. Socrates opened the way to a philosophy of man (*anthropine sophia*); it was Socrates, the man of the streets of Athens, who started the revolution of human ethics on which European philosophy was based. With his death, the Athenian century ended, a few years after Sophocles and Euripides had died, and Athens had lost the war and her imperial position. The tragedies of Socrates and of Athens gave to the century of tragedy a tragic end. The true tragedy was that the very forces which had made Athens great turned against her. The aristocrats disappeared from the scene, and middle-class men rose to the leadership of the state. They could have easily overcome the revolts of the oligarchs, but they could not mend the faults of radical democracy. The civilization of the fourth century was essentially no longer one of citizens, though orators of genius like Demosthenes fought with great vigor the last battle for freedom. Isocrates praised the democracy of the past, but dreamt of Greek unity under a monarch's leadership. Outstanding aristocrats like Plato retired from practical politics and built their new state in Utopia. We may take it as a warning not to overestimate the impact of society on the genius, that of the two greatest men in fourth-century Athens, the one, Plato, was an aristocrat who had lost touch with his own state and people, and the other, Aristotle, was born in Macedon and was at Athens only as Plato's disciple, and later as head of a new philosophical school, yet was to create a system of philosophy and science of worldwide extent. But he no less than Plato, though no Polis-citizen, was looking back to a Polis which was in decline, although they both enjoyed the "academic freedom" of democracy. Even Alexander, whom he taught, did not turn Aristotle's political and social ideas toward the future, toward new forms of state and society. What in contemporary Athens remained of cultural and artistic forces was a legacy looked after and indeed carried on by an unpolitical bourgeoisie. It was those forces whose finest fruit was New Comedy, but they did more than that; they opened the door to a new future, the oecumenic civilization of the Hellenistic Age.

# IV. Republican Rome

The moment we try to speak of society and civilization in Republican Rome, we enter a world completely different from the Greek one. We can distinguish three periods in its history: an early one down to c. 300 B.C., the origins and the firm establishment of Rome from within and without; a second period down to 133 B.C., the great period; and a third one, the time of revolution and decline. In each period we meet with particular difficulties. Early Rome means for the historian a field of little knowledge and widely different modern views, mainly based on new archaeological discoveries or new linguistic evidence. In the middle period, Roman civilization, while under strong Greek influence, shows Roman strength and character at its height, but at the same time infected by the dangerous disease that comes into the open in the last period. The time of the late Republic is the period of the corruption of ancient standards, but also a time of great refinements in life and literature and art. It ends with Caesar and Augustus, and that means with the beginning of the Imperial Age, with which I do not intend to deal. This last lecture of my course will of necessity compress its subject even more and show more shortcomings than the previous lectures; if this sounds like a *captatio benevolentiae* on my part, I can only say: it *is*.

Obviously, Roman civilization did not excel in the same things as Greek civilization. It is equally obvious that there are aspects of it which are purely or almost purely Roman or Italic, and others which would never have been possible without the direct and overwhelming impact of Greek civilization. In its final form, Roman civilization was the first—except for the Mycenaean—to be largely based on another one, and since it was the Greeks who imposed so much of their thought and art on Rome, the latter was the first "European" civilization. Europe came out of Greece via Rome.

We ask first what were the cultural achievements the Romans displayed before the third century B.C. There was the Latin language with its unique capacity for both clarity and brevity. There was the creation of a legal system, both public and private, and the interconnection between law and language. There was, above all, the Roman character with its toughness, its military ability, its strange religious attitude. It is clear that the great achievements, say, of Latin literature or Roman architecture did not simply grow out of the soil of Latium, that the Roman genius found its early expression in other directions. The society of early Rome was a farming society, and despite all later urbanization the true Roman for centuries was a peasant.

Now, peasants seem more or less alike everywhere. But there was a world of difference between the Greek and Roman peasantry. The Latins of whom the Romans were part had a long and important prehistory; but when they began to shape their own history they had no Homer or Hesiod to speak for them or to teach them; there was only a strict family organization and a narrow religious world. Roman gods were natural forces, many of them evil, not thought of in human shape or in any shape at all. They accompanied or threatened the peasant's life every moment; there was help to be won and there were dangers to be checked, both by elaborate magical rituals. These so-called gods did not live in Heaven or on Mt. Olympus, nor were they forces of the underworld. They lived with men on earth, helping or damaging them, but entirely outside the human sphere. No stories could be told about connections between men and gods; such tales came only with the Greeks. No Roman could ever feel, as the Greeks did, an encouraging closeness to a divine person. There were no divine persons; there were legends, but there was no mythology. *Religio* was not a matter of belief, but was the ability to secure good relations with the supernatural forces, and was closely linked with the political community. The rules of the game were first in the hands of the powerful *pater familias,* and from house and family the circle widened to cover the community. A man was *pius* when he served the traditional religious and social order in family and state. The function, for instance, of keeping the home fire burning was transferred to the state and given to the Vestal Virgins, originally children under ten. There were gods locally bound up with the community, such as Ianus, guardian of the city gates or—after a new interpretation—of water crossings, or Quirinus, the warlike protector of the *Quirites* who—as *co-virites*—were the predecessors of the *populus Romanus.* The priestly collegium of the *pontifices* guarded the secrets of rituals, and thus of law as well. The name *pontifices* (bridge- or path-builders) remains enigmatic, as does the proverb *sexagenarios de ponte.* Frazer's definition of the *pontifices* as "a cross between theologians and civil engineers" begs the question; in truth, they were neither the one nor the other. But they upheld the narrow legalistic conservatism of Roman religion, which was equaled only by the ease with which foreign cults were later accepted, as a result of Rome's relations with the Greeks and the East. On the whole, the divine world with which the early Romans lived, and which knew of no statues or temples, was one of superstitious peasant-warriors; there is hardly any indication of craft or trade in connection with the many sacred rules and taboos. The Romans were brought up to a life of work on the land and service to the community, both in peace and in war.

The religious world was, as it were, identical with the social world. After a long prehistory, which is important but outside the purpose of my lectures, several villages on the hills had combined to form one community, probably that of the Septimontium. When that happened we do not know; the early seventh century seems the most likely period. But it was the Etruscans who introduced urban life. Rome is an Etruscan name; that city belonged to the late seventh or early sixth century. It was surrounded by the sacred furrow (*pomerium*) according to Etruscan ritual. The *cloaca maxima* was built to drain the Forum swamps; walls surrounded the city. Tusculum and other Etruscan place names point to a lengthy occupation of Latium (and indeed Campania) by the Etruscans, and Rome then was only one of several small Latin communities. It is possible that much of the tradition of early political activity and power was annalistic invention in *maiorem Romae gloriam,* and that for quite a time Rome stood under the shadow of Etruscan Veii across the river. Still, it became a center of roads, situated as it was between the Italo-Etruscan civilization in the North and the Italo-Campanian in the South, both nourished by Greek traditions of great strength. Obviously, the small community south of the Tiber, even when able to gather the Latins on their side, could never think of putting up a civilization independent of those advanced civilizations in North and South. The hard-working, superstitious peasants of Latium might stick to their practical, no-nonsense mentality, but they could not help receiving a continuous and various impact from the outside, both in people and in ideas. The Latin alphabet was—directly or via the Etruscans—an offspring of the Chalcidian alphabet of Cumae; it was accepted before the sixth century. The famous *fibula* from Praeneste (late seventh century) was Etruscan, but has a Latin inscription in a very ancient alphabet (see fig. 28); it runs: *Manios med fhefhaked Numasioi* (i.e., *Manius me (fe)fecit Numerio*—Manius made me for Numerius). It is like a symbol of the struggling early Latin world and the unity of the three main elements of Roman civilization: Italic, Etruscan, Greek. There are other early inscriptions, among them the famous sacred law of the *Lapis Niger* on the Forum. All the time some new archaeological evidence is forthcoming, but as far as I know, there is very little to show trade or deeper cultural relations with the Greeks before the sixth century. The art of writing was most willingly accepted and was soon to be of special importance; but, taken as a whole, there was a self-sufficiency about early Rome and Latium which asks for more explanation.

It could easily be understood if it had been just a condition of prehistoric primitiveness, as with some of the other Italic peoples. But Rome's growing union with the Latins proves early political and military strength; the Latin Diana of Aricia was supplanted by the federal Diana on the Aventine. Moreover, the history of Roman law shows an early, well-developed body of customary law long before it was written down, and the political institutions had gone far beyond the stage of primitive village or tribal life. The story of the kings, as told by the annalists from the third century onward, is a patriotic legend, given its final shape, though not without some skepticism, by Livy. It is one of the most discussed questions to what extent the legends contain a nucleus of historical truth. Hypercriticalness is no longer the fashion. Though no detail can be taken for certain, unless confirmed by other evidence, there must have been some genuine tradition, preserved partly perhaps in a chronicle kept by the *pontifices* and reflected in various religious rituals, to a greater extent by written family traditions and those of religious brotherhoods like the *Fratres Arvales,* but above all by stories handed down from father to son by word of mouth.

The field where true retrospective conclusions are most likely to be gained is that of law. The organization of government in the early republic grew out of a monarchy in which some noble families had learned to serve the state. After the expulsion of the last king, the regal power was divided among republican officials, but they held even as colleagues the undivided power of *imperium,* which was basically military. The necessary division between peace and war was stressed by the change of clothes when the magistrate crossed the *pomerium;* Rome gave a legal and constitutional meaning to the Etruscan ritual by separating the areas of *domi* and *militiae,* of home and abroad—in practice often of peace and war. There never was a community in which nonbureaucratic officials were so powerful; they were rightly called magistrates because they were more (*magis*) than ordinary citizens, and yet as annual office-holders they depended on the senate, once the advisers to the king; its decrees were still regarded, at least in theory, as advices to the magistrates. The people gained gradually a modest influence in their assemblies, but that is mainly a later story. Without the strength of her inner, essentially aristocratic structure Rome would never have succeeded in becoming the mistress of Italy and in creating a Latin civilization.

In civil law all procedure was originally oral. In *iudex* and *iudicium, condicio,* and *interdictum* the root of *dicere* is still manifest, and otherwise strict adherence to *certa verba* is necessary to complete the symbolic legal action. The astonishing thing is not that law started with oral procedure, but that it was already a complex system that retained its essential features all through the codification and interpretation of the following centuries. Most legal concepts, especially in property and family law, were fixed before magisterial jurisdiction introduced written procedure. It is probably true to say that law was the greatest achievement of early Roman civilization.

At its back, however, was the Latin language, an instrument not of poetical expansiveness but of precise and logical brevity. It incorporated and adapted Mediterranean, Greek, and Etruscan words into a new unity. For us that early stage is preserved in a few inscriptions and quotations, but it is easy to realize that the chief training ground of language was legislation and jurisdiction. The collegium of the *pontifices* held law, language, and ritual together; while *ius* ruled the community, *fas* was the code of what was allowed to man in his relations with the supernatural. Later, the purely legal importance of the *pontifices* slowly decreased, though it never entirely ceased. As the body in charge of the oral tradition, and afterward the archives, they were also responsible for a simple form of chronicle.

The pontifices were originally appointed by the king and taken from the families of the *patricii,* whose fathers (*patres*) were prominent among the community. They were farmers like the rest, though they belonged to the well-to-do. An aristocratic trend was manifest even in the earliest Roman society. The education of the young was essentially one of moral values, and the examples were taken from the national past. The noble families owned the larger estates. There is interesting archaeological evidence. Underground galleries have been found in Latium and Etruria, a complicated and expensive system to irrigate the plains. It must have been carried out by the combined efforts of groups of landowners, some of whom at least must have been wealthy. A peculiar survival of this early situation is the word *rivalis* that first meant a man living near a stream or canal; neighborhood along such an invaluable waterway did not always lead to friendly relations, but often led to rivalry. The smaller farmers were more or less dependent; perhaps the institution of clientele goes back to those early times.

During the sixth century, if not earlier, Rome came under Etruscan rule. The Romans succumbed to their new masters' advanced civilization in which native-Italic, Greek, and Oriental elements were mixed. A statue like the Apollo of Veii—the town from which the Tarquins imported official sculpture—reveals how the Romans were suddenly confronted with gods in human shape and a highly sophisticated, if eclectic art. Another example of this art is the eternal symbol of Rome, the bronze she-wolf (fig. 29). Religious and cultural Etruscan influence can hardly be overestimated, and through the medium of Etruscan civilization the influence of Greek art grew stronger. Etruscan sculpture of the sixth century shows Aeneas with his father Anchises on his back; the derivation from Troy was a very ancient story. The time was not very far off when literature and art could no longer be excluded from Roman life. It is the more remarkable that law and language emerged from the Etruscan period practically unscathed in their original character. Otherwise the Romans were never again quite the same people. Their calendar was largely Etruscan, and so was the ceremony of the triumph. The temple on the Capitol with its triad, Jupiter, Juno, and Minerva, was Etruscan, and probably replaced an earlier Latin triad, Romulus, Mars, and Quirinus. In their dread of evil supernatural forces, the Romans had developed a system of their own, by observing the flight of birds or by other means, to find out what the prospects of an intended action might be; that was the *augurium,* and a body of priests served as augurs. Later the state accepted as well an intricate system of foretelling the future by the Etruscan *haruspices* who interpreted the livers of sacrificial victims. These few facts may suffice to indicate the fundamental mixture on which the cultural influence of the Greeks was to play. We understand why the question could be raised whether Roman civilization was original or derivative. There is no simple straightforward answer to that.

The heads of the small number of patrician families who had served under the kings and were responsible for the expulsion of the Etruscans were truly *patres* of the state. But for almost two centuries after Rome had become a republic, they, the patricians, had to fight, and gradually give way to, the *plebs* of small farmers, clients, and artisans, most of whom served in the army and thus had a large share in Rome's growing power over her neighbors in Latium, South Etruria, and Campania. The "Struggle of the Orders," as it is called, was a social and political revolution, but never was a revolution fought within more legal terms. Secessions took the place of riots; popular leaders, the *tribuni plebis,* were recognized as sacrosanct by the patricians; and one state office after another was opened to men who had neither the religious nor the political traditions hitherto regarded as necessary. Even the college of the pontifices was eventually half plebeian. A state within the state gradually swallowed up the patrician state; that is how Rome for all times was saved from mob rule. A new ruling class, the *nobilitas,* emerged consisting of both patrician and plebeian families, of whom at least one member had held highest office. *Stirpem nobilitavit honor* (office gave nobility to our family), we read in the grave inscription of one of the Scipios of the second century B.C. (Dessau, no. 6), and his was an old patrician family! The *nobilitas* soon became as exclusive as the patricians had been. The soldiers who conquered all Italy and defeated Pyrrhus and Hannibal were the *populus Romanus,* the nominal sovereign; but rule by the people—what the Greeks called democracy—was as far away as ever, in spite of each citizen's *ius provocationis,* the right of appeal to the people against any decision by a magistrate, in spite of the tribunician veto, in spite of the expansion of citizenship. An occasional *homo novus* among the senatorial class, a man from outside the noble families, was the exception which confirmed the rule—in this case the rule of the nobility.

The most important event in the long struggle between patricians and plebeians was the codification of law in the *leges duodecim tabularum,* the XII Tables, by which the plebs achieved equal status before the law. This was in the middle of the fifth century, but nothing in the laws (though they are only partially extant) seems really to confirm the story that the commission charged with the legislation sent some of its members to Athens to study Solon's laws. Essentially, it was a truly Roman code of law, the law of a rustic people, an unsystematic collection of traditional and new rules intended to secure a peaceful social atmosphere. It was at the same time written in a monumental and most disciplined language. I give a few examples (Bruns, p. 15ff.). The first law on procedure is: *si in ius vocat ito, ni it antestamino, igitur em capito.* In English, as far as a translation is possible: "If a man calls another before court, he must go. If he does not go, he is to call him as a witness. Thus he has to seize him." Other examples: *si pater filium ter venum duvit, filius a patre liber esto* (IV.2). Emancipation of a grown-up son could only be achieved by a thrice-repeated sale into slavery. The formidable power of the *pater familias* is obvious, but a loophole was given. Or, *si membrum rupsit, ni cum eo pacit, talio esto* (VIII.2). The talio rule—an eye for an eye—still exists, unless the guilty can pacify the injured. The wording makes it quite clear that an agreement, a pact, could be concluded; in most cases that will have happened. Or, *patronus si clienti fraudem fecerit sacer esto* (VIII.21). This shows strong protection of a client against a fraudulent citizen patron. *Sacer* means "dedicated to the gods," "accursed," "outside the law." Religion provided the means of helping the weak. Much more could be quoted, but it will be clear even now that the Roman genius of compromise and realism had created an instrument of the highest quality and the most far-reaching consequences. Social peace did not come at once, but the foundations had been laid.

The XII Tables were the basis of all later jurisprudence in Rome. The Romans, different from the Greeks, did not aim at an abstract justice; they knew of no law of nature. They interpreted, as occasions arose, the laws of the XII Tables which had set the standard. The successors of the pontifices in this respect were either private legal experts who gave advice in their *responsa,* or the praetors who, on account of their *imperium,* created law by their edicts. Many economic laws were promulgated, mostly in favor of the small peasants, though sometimes also of big creditors. Again and again we find that the decisive authority was with the legal tradition that represented the interest of the *res publica.* Even the agrarian and luxury laws of the Gracchi and later reformers were essentially traditional. It is understandable that the interest of the state often meant the interest of a political group, that laws were influenced, if not dictated, by day-to-day politics. Sometimes a scandal was the cause of a new law, and it was just as likely that the law tried to cover the scandalous events so as to make a repetition impossible. From the point of view of abstract morality, Roman legislation and jurisprudence were frequently at fault, and a nineteenth-century liberal like Mommsen accused the Roman jurists of hypocrisy. Meanwhile we have learnt to look at these things rather differently. The Roman virtues of *fides* and *pietas* depended on loyalty to tradition, to the standards set by the ancestors. Ennius' words, often quoted, are generally relevant, although they may have been used by him foremost for military discipline: *moribus antiquis res stat Romana virisque* (*Annales,* fr. 500 V)—"ancient rules and the men to carry them out preserve the state." It was legal to take the traditional forms for any actual purpose; the question of justice did not really arise. It needed a completely new age, when the Republic had gone and the emperor was the final source of law, to bring into being that classical jurisprudence that accepted the Greek philosophy of justice and thus discovered the standards that were to determine legislation deep into the Christian centuries.

Tradition ruled education as well. A censorial edict as late as 92 B.C. (Bruns, no. 67) ordered that no new methods were to be used in children's schools; nothing was to be taught *praeter consuetudinem ac morem maiorum.* Plautus (*Mostell.* 126) said of parents as the *fabri liberum,* the "makers of their children": *docent litteras iura leges,* "they teach reading and writing, judgments and laws." The *leges* were the XII Tables, the *iura* must have been judicial decisions. The former had probably been the chief text used in school; the judgments will later have been added. We may shake our heads at what the Romans regarded a suitable school syllabus; but it was not in school, it was under the guidance of the parents, that is, in the tradition of house and family, that the boys were taught.

During the third and second centuries Greek influence on the Roman upper class became almost overwhelmingly strong. Even so, whatever the form of a cultural achievement, the spirit remained essentially Roman, and that meant bound to the service of the *res publica.* The rustic, realistic, political Roman mind can be detected under any foreign dress. Take the Sibylline books that played such an important part in Roman politics. They were a collection of oracles in Greek; they opposed the Etruscan ways of prophesying; they might easily have introduced not only Greek gods (as they did) but also the Greek views on divine leadership. Nothing of the sort happened; the oracles remained under the control of the pontifices and the state. Or take the Eleusinian triad of Demeter, Kore, and Dionysus; we have instead as early as 493 B.C. Ceres, Liber, and Libera, the first an agrarian deity fashioned after Demeter, the two others a couple, and that means in Roman religion two expressions of the same divine force; Liber was not simply Dionysus. The third century saw the creation of a number of divine abstractions, such as Virtus, Fides, Pietas, Libertas—all of them without a Greek equivalent, all of them powers determining the life of the Roman citizens.

The same third century witnessed the birth of Latin literature. There had been some preliterary Latin poetry, chiefly magical verses, prayers, and ritual songs. They all were called *carmina,* and mostly chanted in a definite meter, the ancient Italic Saturnian verse (I cannot believe in its alleged Greek origin) of which Ennius (fr. 213 V) says that it once was used by *Fauni vatesque,* demons of the woods and human seers. The XII Tables speak of *qui malum carmen incantassit* (VIII.1), obviously the use of a pernicious magic spell. Cato (*Orig.* 118) knows—and Varro (*De vita populi Romani* in Nonius 77.2) repeats it in a partly contradictory form—that *multis saeculis ante suam aetatem,* long before his own time, the participants of a banquet used to sing the praise of famous men to flute accompaniment. This passage was the basis of B. G. Niebuhr's famous reconstruction of early Roman history. There we might have conditions similar to those from which epic poetry sprang in Greece. This analogy, however, makes Cato's statement subject to suspicion; perhaps those scholars are right who deny its truth. Anyway, the tradition, if it had existed, died an early death.

When after the first Punic War Livius Andronicus, a Greek from Tarentum, began to translate the *Odyssey* and to write

Latin plays, he used the Saturnian for the epic, but otherwise adopted and adapted Greek meters; in content and form he generally followed Greek models, though stage and actors of a kind had been known at Rome from Etruscan times. If Andronicus introduced the Saturnian into literature, he laid at the same time the Greek foundations of Latin literature. It is likely that he came to Rome as a prisoner of the Pyrrhic war, and was set free by some Livius. He taught Greek and Latin in Rome, probably mainly poetry. Some Romans of the upper class loved Greece, though none of them could be called hellenized; translations must have been very useful. Andronicus was, as far as I know, the first translator in the general history of literature; he was (as few translators are) a poet as well. His tragedies and comedies were performed at the annual *ludi Romani* or other *ludi* as a form of higher entertainment; they were translations of classical Attic plays, but there was neither a religious background as in Greece nor an inner connection between play and audience. The *Odyssey* looked like a true Latin poem, and its contents of adventure and fairy tale was to delight Roman youth. *Virum mihi Camena insece versutum* is the famous first line, an excellent version from the Greek into new meter and language; *insece* (a word repeated by Ennius in *his* address to the Muse) is an equivalent in sound and meaning of the Greek *ennepe*. Camena is the Italic name of a water nymph which Andronicus raised for all times to the meaning of Muse.

He also saw to the practical side of his stage work, which was not published in book form during his lifetime. He created a *collegium scribarum et histrionum*. The Greek Dionysiac *technitai,* a guild of actors, was known everywhere; the Roman guild followed the example and had its center in the temple of Minerva on the Aventine; she was the goddess of artisans. Roman drama from the beginning was in the hands of craftsmen; *scriba* was certainly not a high-sounding title for a poet. The actors were mostly slaves, and their master was actor as well as producer, an important person who could—like Ambivius Turpio, the producer of all of Terence's plays—influence public taste and the success of the poet. Of Andronicus' guild nothing further is known; we may doubt whether later poets still belonged to it, unless they were actors as well. There was hardly the need of a special center for literary activity, even with the quarrels and polemics still evident from later poetry. Gradually, the magistrates responsible for the *ludi,* the *aediles,* took a hand in the organization; thus the state recognized the existence of a Latin stage.

If Andronicus was essentially a translator, Naevius, Ennius, and Plautus were Latin poets. They were Italic by origin, like most later poets (Terence even came from Africa); they all were Roman by choice and attachment. But they all called themselves *poeta,* borrowing the Greek word. They wished no longer to be either *scriba* or *vates,* the one being too much of a mere craftsman, the other of an inspired man, but not one of Greek culture. Naevius, who had fought in the Roman army during the First Punic War, was indeed imprisoned for attacks on Roman noblemen, and died in exile. His epic on that war, written in Saturnians, was more or less contemporary with the work of Fabius Pictor, a Roman aristocrat who wrote on Roman history in Greek, that is to say, for Greek readers, just as the Babylonian Berossus and the Egyptian Manetho had done for their countries not much earlier. Fabius' idea clearly was to defend Roman policy against Greek misrepresentation. Naevius did even more. He also wrote tragedies and comedies, and at least some of them contained Roman subjects. The *praetexta* and the *togata,* Roman tragedies and comedies called after the dress of senators or citizens, made their first, though for the time only ephemeral, appearance. Of Naevius we have too few fragments to know his work well, but they are sufficient to show that he was a bold innovator. When he accepted as the beginning of Roman history the flight of Aeneas from Troy, when we feel his pride in the deeds of the Roman army or his insistence on *libera lingua,* we realize that there were good patriots who might become opponents of the ruling nobility.

There was, however, no future in Roman literature that was not chiefly based on Greek achievements, as it was realized, or at least practiced, by Naevius' two younger contemporaries, Ennius and Plautus. The former came from Messapia near Tarentum and had a Greek education which gave him the knowledge of both classical and Hellenistic literature. He claimed to have three mother tongues (*tria corda,* three hearts, he calls it): Greek, Oscan, and Latin. As the native Italic languages were gradually overcome by Latin, there remained the bilingual ability which became the sign of the educated Roman. It was a curious coincidence that Ennius, who lived through the Hannibalic war and Rome's expansion afterward, was brought to Rome by Cato, the old-fashioned, self-righteous Roman who learned Greek in his thirties and realized the importance and even more the danger of Greek literature and philosophy. Ennius introduced both to Rome. He wrote tragedies and a great many books, partly in prose and largely reproductions from the Greek. His claim to immortality, however, rests on his *Annales,* an epic poem written in hexameters, a meter which had to be adapted to the Latin language. In the Greek manner he addressed the Muses who were dancing on Mt. Olympus (*quae pedibus magnum pulsatis Olympum,* fr. 1 V). The Latin poet accepted the Greek gods and their mountain home. He even reported a dream in which the shade of Homer told him that his soul survived in Ennius; *Homerum sibi dicentem quod eius anima in suo esset corpore,* says a scholiast. Such concepts were entirely un-Roman, and Ennius had to explain them by a lengthy elaboration of the Pythagorean doctrine of the migration of souls. Not even Virgil called himself another Homer, but Ennius wanted to establish the claim of Roman poetry as equal to the greatest of all possible predecessors. He wrote of the *res gestae* not so much of the Roman people as of outstanding leaders. In that as well as in other features he shows a spirit similar to that of Hellenistic literature, and there are real purple passages, full of rhetoric and verbal devices, among them frequent alliteration, which, however, was Roman, not Greek. Ennius' great poem no less than his other literary activity was to appeal to the most educated Romans. With his emancipated views on religion—he translated Euhemerus and did not even except Iuppiter Optimus Maximus as once having been a human king—he influenced men like the elder Scipio. Deeply impressed by the great events of his own time, Ennius wrote his historical epic with the help of official records, and of stories he heard from Romans and non-Romans; he had also the advantage of writing after Naevius, whom he despised. One of the most remarkable passages still extant is a speech by Pyrrhus (fr. 194ff. V); the king is depicted with admiration for his chivalry. We do not forget that many of Ennius' countrymen fought under Pyrrhus, but his words, in returning Roman prisoners, sound like those coming from a great Roman such as Scipio: "Whose *virtus* the fortune of war has spared, their freedom I shall certainly spare." In his aim of producing Latin poetry equal to the Greek, he almost shared Cato's attitude. However justified or not his claims as a great poet were, the fact that he made them shows that he paved the way for a literature generally above that of the contemporary Greeks. Latin literature had begun to reflect the greatness of Rome, that is the exploits mainly of the nobility.

On the other end of the social scale stands Plautus, actor and writer of comedies (like his late successor Molière), the first Roman poet of whose work a large part has been preserved. His concentration on one kind of poetry shows the breakthrough of a strong personality; it also proves that a writer of comedy could earn a living. Plautus' dependence on Greek New Comedy is well known. His versions of the originals contain much of his own, whether Roman or Italic (*Plautinisches im Plautus* is the significant title of an important book on the poet), but this had nothing to do with politics or war or the ruling class. Comedies were entertainment for ordinary people who were used to local farce, crude witticisms, song, music, and dance. The refined Terence had to fight against the competition of gladiators, pugilists and rope dancers, an atmosphere entirely alien to New Comedy and its sophisticated audience. Still, it remains a fact that the scene and the plot of Plautus' plays were Greek; much of the life and the mind of the Greek bourgeoisie was preserved. This may have attracted those Greek or partially Greek elements who formed a considerable section of the lower classes in Rome. Many of them were freedmen or slaves, and slaves play a far greater part in Plautus than in New Comedy. For the peculiar role of Plautus' comedies it is significant that Greek words and jokes come almost exclusively from persons of low standing. Greek had first entered Rome as something familiar to traders and slaves; we know that Greek slaves frequently taught the youth of the Roman upper class. New vistas, however, were opened by Plautus for the Latin language, which he used with astonishing mastery.

Life in Rome, even of the nobility, had long been very simple. The elder Pliny (*HN* 33.142) tells the story of the Carthaginian ambassadors (probably early in the third century) who were invited to many houses and everywhere

found the same table silver; it had been lent from one family
to the other. Real interest in the beauty of things began with
the capture of Syracuse in 212, and in the following decades,
especially after the sack of Corinth in 146, great wealth, and
with it Greek art and artists, poured into Rome. Ever after,
the houses of the rich were crowded with originals and copies
of Greek sculpture; it is known that artists in Greece were
working for export to Rome. In 155 the famous philosophers'
embassy arrived, and their speeches in Greek attracted large
audiences. Poets like Terence, who has been called as well-
tempered as Menander, and the tragedian Pacuvius, who
largely used Hellenistic plays as his models, also testify to
the Hellenization of Roman education. Scipio Aemilianus
and his friendship with Polybius and Panaetius, and the
growing impact of Stoic philosophy, which suited but
changed the Roman character, all this is the crowning of the
process, in which in Horace's famous words *Graecia capta
ferum victorem cepit et artes intulit agresti Latio* (*Epist.*
2.1.156). Hellenized Rome finally broke with its rustic past.
Lucilius, the only poet of high social standing, belonged to
the circle round Aemilianus and wrote poetry in the way of
personal talks among friends, with sharp and frank invective,
both political and literary; under the name of *satura* this
became indeed a purely Roman form of poetry.

The elder Cato was always considered, and in many ways
was, the example of an "old Roman." In his long life (234–
149) he experienced the invasion of Greek civilization and
the beginning of the decline of Roman moral standards.
Against these "modern" trends he fought with passionate
stubbornness; but in spite of his contempt for the *Graeculi*
he could not help learning from them. He was not the first
to write literary Latin prose, which had grown up in the
traditions of law and public speaking; but he was the first to
take the task seriously. Owing to the large amount he wrote

and to his powerful personality, he was read for a long time; thus we have enough preserved to know him, though only one book (*de agri cultura*) is completely extant. That is a handbook for the gentleman farmer, written in factual and impressive short sentences. Agriculture—which meant, above all, the growing of vines and olive trees and well irrigated gardens—is the best occupation possible, better than risky trade and dishonest money-lending. "Our ancestors, if they wanted to praise a *vir bonus,* praised him as a *bonus agricola bonusque colonus.*" With trade and finance, Cato mentions the main occupations of the middle class of *equites,* which had superseded the original class of the highest equestrian aristocracy and at that time came into its own by acquiring enormous wealth and increasing political influence. It was the class Cato himself came from, but he remained a countryman, and for him, as for the senators whose ranks he joined, land was the only legitimate source of income. Accordingly he describes the work of the owner of a medium estate as a source of material gains, without any sentimentality for rural life and little concern for the slaves working for him. Despite its austerity, the book shows Cato as a man of his century, a century seized by the spirit of money-making.

Other books were written by Cato for the education of his son to avoid the use of Greek books, which Cato himself had thoroughly studied. There was even a book on rhetoric, not theoretical and formal as a Greek would have written it, but practical. A *vir bonus* must be *dicendi peritus,* and the whole art of speaking is contained in the slogan *rem tene, verba sequentur* ("hold firm the matter, and the words will follow"). Cato followed here an ancient Roman tradition. On the Forum as well as in the Senate the Roman leaders learned to make speeches. We can be sure that there was a Roman practice of rhetoric long before Greek theory and practice had had their full impact. Naevius and Plautus quite frequently use rhetorical devices, and these, more likely than not, grew out of Italic soil and Roman city life. Cato kept an archive of his own speeches; the fragments show his forceful language, especially in those delivered when he was censor; he denounced members of the nobility in the most violent terms, attacks that led to passionate feuds within the Senate, in particular with Scipio Africanus and his followers. The decline of the unity, and thus of the power, of the ruling class had started.

The greatest of Cato's works, however, was his history of Rome, called *Origines,* although only the first three out of seven books dealt with the origins of Rome and other Italic cities. The latter topic is important: Cato was not an urban Roman, and he regarded the whole of Italy, even including the Transpadani, who became citizens only a century later, as a unit; this was a conception far ahead of his time. Cato's work was not a chronicle, as he says himself, like the *tabula apud pontificem maximum* with its records of sun and moon eclipses and famines. He wrote the heroic history of the Roman people. For that reason he left out all individual names, though it must be said that in the later books his own deeds did play a prominent part. The union between Roman state and Greek thought in Cato was curiously cramped and unbalanced, while it reached full harmony in Scipio Aemilianus.

The Roman mind, whether in foreign dress or not, always centered on state and people. I have pointed out that the nature of Roman jurisprudence was largely determined by its use in the service of the state. Ennius created in Greek shape a national Roman epic. Plautus transformed Greek comedies to please his Roman audiences. Recently it has been shown that Roman art, in an eclecticism at the beginning rather than at the end of its history, expressed the social and political spirit of Rome and her rulers, and no aesthetic ideals. It is never right to judge one civilization by the standards of another, even when it largely derives from it; that is why it is a mistake to take Roman literature or art as a sort of degenerated or petrified repetition of Greek achievements. To put our mind right, we must only think of architecture. It is, of course, significant that Roman independence can above all be seen in that art that was technical and practical. It is symptomatic that the Romans were never quite at ease in recognizing art as something one ought to know about. There were many good craftsmen, but hardly ever outstanding artists among the Romans. When Rome's water supply had to be organized, the Aqua Appia was built as early as 312 B.C., mainly underground like the ancient galleries, but bridges had also to be built, and with the new tasks new techniques were discovered. In the second century masonry arches were built for bridges and aqueducts, and with them Roman architecture embarked on a road which led to vaults and domes, and thus to buildings never dreamt of by the Greeks. It was also an Italic tradition that determined town planning with the dominating position of civic buildings. Temples were not self-contained like the Greek ones, but turned their faces, real façades, toward forum and public life.

There is only one branch of pure art in which the Romans excelled, the human portrait. We meet naturalistic heads of men and women in Etruscan art (see figs. 30, 31). In addition to this influence, Roman noble families kept the death masks of their ancestors made in wax, which would be carried in funeral processions. Easily destroyed, they soon were copied in terracotta or bronze. Genuine portraiture was the next step, though it would not have been taken without the knowledge of contemporary Hellenistic art. Some of the earlier Roman portraits (see fig. 32) (the dating of which, unfortunately, differs widely among modern archaeologists) show impressive heads of rustic *gravitas,* sometimes of more —intellectual sharpness or wily slyness. From here began a Roman tradition that was revived in the Renaissance.

Most of these portraits belong to the period of the late Republic, to the time of Cicero and Lucretius. Cicero, not a great statesman but better than his reputation among schoolboys, was the most universal mind among the Romans; his books made him the strongest force in European education. Lucretius proclaimed Epicurean philosophy as the way of liberation from the fear of death and from the belief in the supernatural; his prophetic soul had the fervor of Greeks such as Parmenides or Empedocles. Art and literature alike revealed a strong individualism. They can be understood only against the background of a widely disrupted society. The growth of latifundia and slave labor, the distress of the small farmer, the discontent of the Italian allies, the rise of a wealthy nonsenatorial class, the poverty of the urban masses, the corruption among the ruling class, the ruthless ambition of individual leaders and the land hunger of the veterans, finally perhaps also the gap between the educated and the uneducated, all this brought about the age of revolution and civil war, when loyalty to the state was often only a hypocritical phrase. I have no room to describe the decline of the Republic at any length; as this period and its representatives are much better known than the earlier ones, I feel I can be very brief.

The Roman poets and writers of the last century B.C. have in common a full awareness of Greek civilization and the strength of their own genius, Roman but individual. The society of the age which included the two *ordines,* the senatorial class and that of the *equites,* was not only completely divided by political and personal strife, but with a few exceptions had also broken with the ancient traditions. Family was still an instrument of politics, but family life hardly existed. Women were emancipated, partly legally, even more so in their private existence. Men and women alike lived dissolute lives; adultery and divorce were as frequent as pederasty. The passionate love of Catullus for his Lesbia, who was Clodia and thus of patrician stock, reveals her immorality in a striking contrast to his genuine feelings. With him erotic poetry reached a height and a frankness hardly ever surpassed. If this was the upper class, the ordinary people had practically lost all interest in public life, and were chiefly concerned with the food question and crude entertainments: *panem et circenses.*

The greatest man of the age, representative in his outstanding genius as in his lack of moral and traditional standards, was Caesar. His attempt to end the death struggle of the Republic by imposing his autocratic will was bound to fail. With Augustus a true reaction and revival started, by no means fully successful; but it was he who brought peace to the Roman world, and with it a new atmosphere in which Virgil, Horace, and Livy could live and write. Augustus claimed with some justification to have restored the *res publica,* but the Republic was dead, if not yet buried. Roman society developed into a completely new organism, and Roman civilization, spreading through and even beyond the empire, soared to heights hitherto unknown, leaving its monuments all over the world.

# SELECTED
# BIBLIOGRAPHY

# INDEX

# Selected Bibliography

Mentioning or not mentioning a book or article in this bibliography does not imply a verdict on my part, either favorable or unfavorable. I merely wish to name works which have proved useful to me and which, at the same time, may be useful for those who want to penetrate more deeply into the questions involved. In each section, the titles are given in alphabetical order. Ancient texts are not mentioned here, nor are general histories of Greece or Rome.

## Lectures I–IV

Adkins, A. W. H., *Merit and Responsibility* (Oxford: Clarendon Press, 1960).

Bonnard, A., *Greek Civilization,* vols. I–III (London: Allen & Unwin, 1957–1961).

Bowra, C. M., *The Greek Experience* (London: Weidenfeld & Nicolson, 1957).

Ehrenberg, V., *The Greek State* (Oxford: B. Blackwell, 1960).

Festugiere, A. J., *Personal Religion among the Greeks,* Sather Classical Lectures (Berkeley: University of California Press, 1954).

Fränkel, H., *Dichtung und Philosophie des frühen Griechentums,* 2 ed. (Munich: C. H. Beck, 1961).

Gomme, A. W., *More Essays in Greek History and Literature* (Oxford: B. Blackwell, 1962).

Guthrie, W. K. C., *The Greeks and Their Gods* (London: Methuen & Co., 1950).

Jaeger, W., *Paideia,* vols. I–III, and 4 ed. (Berlin: de Gruyter, 1959). English edition (Oxford: B. Blackwell, 1939–1945).

Lesky, A., *Geschichte der griechischen Literatur,* 2 ed. (Berne: Franke, 1963). An English edition is forthcoming.

Marrou, H.-I., *Histoire de l'éducation dans l'antiquité* (Paris: Editions du Seuil, 1950); English edition (London: Sheed & Ward, 1956).

Pearson, L., *Popular Ethics in Ancient Greece* (Palo Alto: Stanford University Press, 1962).

Rohde, E., *Psyche,* 5 and 6 ed. (Tubingen: Mohr, 1910).

Snell, B., *Die Entdeckung des Geistes,* 3 ed. (Hamburg: Claaszen & Goverts, 1955); English edition (Oxford: B. Blackwell, 1953, from second German edition).

――――*Poetry and Society,* Patten Lectures (Bloomington: Indiana University Press, 1961).

Starr, C. G., *The Origins of Greek Civilization* (New York: Knopf, 1961).

Wade-Gery, H. T., *Essays in Greek History* (Oxford: B. Blackwell, 1958).

## Lecture I

Bowra, C. M., *Heroic Poetry* (Oxford: Clarendon Press, 1952).

Burn, A. R., *The World of Hesiod* (London: Kegan Paul, Trench, Trubner & Co., 1936).

Else, G. F., "Origin of *Tragodia,*" *Hermes* 85:17–46 (1957).

Finley, I. M., *The World of Odysseus* (London: Chatto & Windus, 1956).

Heuss, A., "Die archaische Zeit Griechenlands als geschichtliche Epoche," in *Antike und Abendland,* vol. II (Hamburg: M. v. Schroeder, 1946), pp. 26–62.

Jeffrey, H., *The Local Scripts of Archaic Greece* (Oxford: Oxford University Press, 1961).

Kirk, G. S., *The Songs of Homer* (Cambridge, Eng.: Cambridge University Press, 1962).

Latte, K., "Hesiods Dichterweihe," in *Antike und Abendland,* vol. II (Hamburg: M. v. Schroeder, 1946), pp. 152–163.

Lord, A. B., *The Singer of Tales* (Cambridge, Mass.: Harvard University Press, 1960).

Lorimer, H. L., *Homer and the Monuments* (London: Macmillan & Co., 1950).

Page, D. L., *History and the Homeric Iliad,* Sather Classical Lectures (Berkeley: University of California Press, 1959).

Patzer, H., *"Rhapsodos,"* *Hermes* 80:314–325 (1952).

Schadewaldt, W., *Von Homers Welt und Werk,* 3 ed. (Stuttgart: Koehler, 1960).

Ventris, M., and J. Chadwick, *Documents in Mycenaean Greek* (Cambridge, Eng.: Cambridge University Press, 1956).

Vermeule, E. T., "The Fall of the Mycenaean Empire," *Archaeology* 13:66–75 (1960).

Walcot, P., "Hesiod and the Didactic Literature of the Near East," *Revue des études grecques* 75:13–36 (1962).

Webster, T. B. L., *From Mycenae to Homer* (London: Methuen & Co., 1958).

Whitman, C. H., *Homer and the Homeric Tradition* (Cambridge, Mass.: Harvard University Press, 1958).

### Lecture II

Andrewes, A., *The Greek Tyrants* (London: Hutchinson's University Library, 1956).

Bowra, C. M., *Greek Lyric Poetry,* 2 ed. (Oxford: Clarendon Press, 1961).

Burn, A. R., *The Lyric Age of Greece* (London: E. Arnold, 1960).

Defradas, J., "Le banquet de Xénophane," *Revue des études grecques* 75:344–365 (1962).

Dodds, E. R., *The Greeks and the Irrational,* Sather Classical Lectures (Berkeley: University of California Press, 1951).

Dunbabin, T. J., *The Greeks and their Eastern Neighbours* (London: Society for the Promotion of Hellenic Studies, 1957).

Ehrenberg, V., "Der Damos im archaischen Sparta," *Hermes* 68:288–305 (1933).

Flacelière, R., *L'amour en Grèce* (Paris: Hachette, 1960); English edition (London: Fr. Muller, 1962).

Forrest, W. G., "The Tribal Organisation of Chios," *Annual British School at Athens* 55:172–190 (1960).

Homann-Wedeking, E., "Von spartanischer Art und Kunst," in *Antike und Abendland,* vol. VII (Hamburg: M. v. Schroeder, 1958), pp. 63–72.

Jacoby, F., "The Date of Archilochus," *Classical Quarterly* 35:97–109 (1941).

Kirk, G. S., and J. E. Raven, *The Presocratic Philosophers* (Cambridge, Eng.: Cambridge University Press, 1957).

Minto, A., "Il vaso François," in *Accademia Toscana di Scienze e Lettere,* Studi, vol. VI (Florence: Olschki, 1960).

Mylonas, G. E., *Eleusis and the Eleusinian Mysteries* (Princeton: Princeton University Press, 1961).

Page, D. L., *The Parthenion* (Oxford: Clarendon Press, 1951).

Pfeiffer, R., "Gottheit und Individuum in der frühgriechischen Lyrik." *Philologus* 84:137–152 (1925) = *Ausgewählte Schriften* (Munich: C. H. Beck, 1960), pp. 42–54.

*The Mysteries,* Papers from the Eranos Yearbooks (London: Routledge & Kegan, 1955).

Vogt, J., "Von der Gleichwertigkeit der Geschlechter in der bürgerlichen Gesellschaft der Griechen," *Abhandlungen Mainzer Akademie,* 1960.

Webster, T. B. L., *Greek Art and Literature 700–530 B.C.* (London: Methuen & Co., 1959).

### Lecture III

Ehrenberg, V., "Origins of Democracy," *Historia* 1:515–548 (1950–1952).

—— *The People of Aristophanes,* 2 ed. (Oxford: B. Blackwell, 1951); 2 ed., paperback (New York: Schocken Books, 1962).

—— *Sophocles and Pericles* (Oxford: B. Blackwell, 1954); 2 ed. in German (Munich: C. H. Beck, 1956).

Guardini, R., *Der Tod des Sokrates* (Godesberg: H. Küpper, 1947).

Heinimann, F., *Nomos und Physis* (Basel: F. Reinhardt, 1945).

Jones, A. H. M., *Athenian Democracy* (Oxford: B. Blackwell, 1957).

Romilly, J. de., *Histoire et raison chez Thucydide* (Paris: Les Belles Lettres, 1956).

Schaefer, H., "Praktische Ordnung und individuelle Freiheit im Griechentum," *Historische Zeitschrift* 183:5–22 (1957).

Strasburger, H., "Herodot und das perikleische Athen," *Historia* 4:1–25 (1955).

### Lecture IV

Alföldi, A., "Il santuario federale latino di Diana," *Studi e Materiali di Storia della Religione* 32:21–39 (1961).

—— "Ager Romanus Antiquus," *Hermes* 90:187–213 (1962).

Altheim, F., and D. Ferber, *Einzeluntersuchungen zur altitalischen Geschichte* (Frankfurt: Klostermann, 1961).

Bianchi-Bandinelli, R., "Römische Kunst zwei Generationen nach Wickhoff," *Klio* 38:267–289 (1960).

Bloch, R., *Les origines de Rome* (Paris: Club française du Livre, 1959); English edition (New York: Praeger, 1960).

Dahlmann, H., "Zur Ueberlieferung über die 'altrömischen Tafellieder'," *Abhandlungen Mainzer Akademie,* 1950.

Fraccaro, P., "Di alcuni antichissimi lavori idraulici, etc.," *Opuscula,* vol. III.1 (Pavia: Rivista Athenaeum, 1957), pp. 1–49.

—— "The History of Rome in the Regal Period," *Journal of Roman Studies* 47:59–65 (1957).

Fraenkel, E., *Plautinisches im Plautus* (Berlin: Weidmann, 1922).

Frank, T., *An Economic History of Rome,* 2 ed. (New York: Cooper Square Publishers, 1962).

Gjerstad, E., *Legends and Facts of Early Roman History,* Scripta Minora (Lund: Gleerup, 1962).

Grimal, P., *La civilization romaine* (Paris: Arthaud, 1960). An English edition is forthcoming.

Heurgon, J., "L'état étrusque," *Historia* 6:63–97 (1957).

—— *La vie quotidienne chez les Étrusques* (Paris: Hachette, 1961).

Holland, L. A., *Janus and the Bridge* (Rome: American Academy, 1961).

Jachmann, G., *Die Originalität der römischen Literatur,* Inaugural Speech (University of Cologne, 1926).

Kaschnitz-von Weinberg, G., *Das Schöpferische in der römischen Kunst* (Hamburg: Rowohlt, 1961).

Kienast, D., *Cato der Zensor* (Heidelberg: Quelle & Meyer, 1954).

Klingner, F., *Römische Geisteswelt,* 4 ed. (Munich: Ellermann, 1961).

Latte, K., *Römische Religionsgeschichte* (Munich: C. H. Beck, 1960).

Leo, F., *Geschichte der römischen Literatur,* vol. I (Berlin: Weidmann, 1913).

Momigliano, A., "Perizonius and the Character of Early Roman Tradition," *Journal of Roman Studies* 47:104–114 (1957).

Muth, R., "Römische Religio," *Serta Philologica Aenipontana,* Innsbrucker Beiträge zur Kulturwissenschaft, Band 7–8 (1962), pp. 247–271.

Richter, G. M. A., "Greek Portraits," *Coll. Latomus* 20, 36, 48 (1955, 1959, 1960).

Scullard, H. H., *Roman Politics 220–150 B.C.* (Oxford: Clarendon Press, 1951).

Skutsch, O., *The Annals of Quintus Ennius,* Inaugural Speech (London: Lewis & Co., 1953).

Syme, R., *The Roman Revolution* (Oxford: Clarendon Press, 1939).

Wieacker, F., *Vom römischen Recht,* 2 ed. (Stuttgart: Koehler, 1962).

# Index

Achilles, 7, 11, 14
Acropolis Museum, 50
Aeolia, 37
Aeolus, 7
Aeschylus, 57–58; *Persae,* 54–55
Agamemnon, 8
Ages of Man, 14
Ajax, 56
Alcaeus of Lesbos, 26, 30–31, 32, 49
Alcibiades, 68
Alcinous, 9
Alcmaeon of Croton, 47
Alcman, 33–35, 42
Alexander the Great, 69
Alphabet: development of Greek, 17–18; Roman, 71
Ambivius Turpio, 84
Anacreon, 36, 49
Anaxagoras, 40, 58
Anaximander, 37, 38, 47
Anaximenes of Miletus, 37
Aphrodite, 18
Apollines (*Kouroi*), 50
Apollo, 8, 12, 14, 18
Archilochus, 26, 29–30, 31, 32, 42
Arete, 9
Aristocracy: in Archaic Age, 27–28; Athenian, 48–49; Cretan, 5; Roman, 76–78, 86; and singers, 9. *See also* Homeric society
Aristogeiton, 47
Aristophanes: *The Clouds,* 48–49, 66; *The Frogs,* 57; *Lysistrata,* 27
Aristotle, 69
Artemis, 5
Athena: Athenian, 50; Minoan, 5
Athens: in 9th and 8th centuries B.C., 19–22; family life, 59–60; role of

foreigners in, 61–64; vase painting in, 18–22
Augury, 77–78
Augustus, 93

Bards, *see* Singers
Berossus, 84

Caesar, 93
Callinus, 31
Calliope, 13
Cato, 82, 85, 86; influence of Greek on, 88–90; *Origines,* 90
Catullus, 93
Chios: Homerids in, 12; in Archaic Age, 28–29
Choral singing, 33–34, 52; at funerals, 8
Cicero, 92
Cimon, 51, 58
Cleisthenes, 44, 46–47, 52, 62
Clodia, 93
Comedy: Greek, 55; New, 59, 69; Old, 57; Roman, 87, 90. *See also* Theater; Tragedy
Corinth, 29, 37
Cratinus, 58
Crete, 4–6
Critias, 68
Cypselus, 29
Cyrnus, 37

Delian Hymn to Apollo, 12
Delphi, 25, 43
Demeter, 10, 41–42
Demodocus, 8
Demosthenes, 69
Diana, 74